Passive Income

Incredible Ideas of How to Make Money While You Sleep

Part One

Passive Income Series

Part One:

 EBook Writing

 YouTube Ad Revenue

 Stock Photos

 Audio Samples

Part Two:

 Print per Demand

 Instagram

 Creating Online Courses

Part Three:

 P2P Lending

 Creating Apps

 Joint Venture Partnerships

Part Four:

 Selling Your Product or Service

 Affiliate Marketing

 Dividend Stocks

Table of Contents

Introduction

I want to thank you and congratulate you for downloading *Passive Income: Incredible Ideas Of How To Make Money While You Sleep, Part One.*

A few short years ago I was living paycheck to paycheck, and just like many Americans I was in a vicious cycle of work and bills, with little ability to generate savings. The idea of investing for the future seemed like a fairy tale, as if investing was reserved for only the wealthiest among us. The truth is that even average Americans can save for their future through minimal investments. It is in generating passive income that we can lift ourselves out of the cycle of living paycheck to paycheck, and even if this does not describe you in particular, you will be able to further your income through these outside investments.

In part one of a four part series on passive income, you will learn how to supplement your main line of work through passive investments. Do not let the name fool you; these are investments that require up front work for long term payoff. These are investments for the rest of us, and I have designed this guide around my own experiences. You must note that passive income builds on top of previous ventures, and while your starting income stream may seem small, it will increase with time. Passive investments start as active investments and your past efforts will turn into revenue streams for long into the future. There are many guides being sold on passive income, and these will claim that passive income is passive from the very beginning – this simply isn't true. When I consider how other writers describe passive income, I'm left with the thought of a classic example in basic economics: *Two men are walking down a sidewalk. The first man sees a twenty-dollar bill and says to the other that there is money on the sidewalk. The second man does not look down at the ground and simply continues walking. The first man, befuddled, catches up the second and asks, why didn't you pick up the money? The second man replies, if money had truly been left on the sidewalk, it wouldn't be there.*

This parable demonstrates an important lesson about passive income – nothing comes easy. The second man does not waste his time looking for the free money on the sidewalk because he knows that such a good thing could not possibly exist; if money had been there, it would already be gone. Consider this as you build your passive income streams – it requires the up front work, and anyone that tells you anything different is selling a lie, a beautifully attractive one, but a lie nevertheless.

Generating passive income is paramount, but it is especially dire for nearly half of all Americans. This may sound hyperbolic, but a recent 2016 survey shows that nearly half of all households are not prepared for an emergency costing $500 or more. To have so little savings, to be so unprepared for the future, it creates a disaster just waiting to happen. You cannot fault Americans for not saving; our purchasing power has decreased over the last three decades, and the cost of living has only increased. It is for these reasons that investing for passive income seems so impossible for many families.

Over the following chapters you will learn how to generate passive income through investments that can be made entirely from your own home. These are starting investments that require no money to start, and the catalyst for your success is the effort and motivation that you put into these projects. This is the key takeaway for passive income – it requires up front work for long term payoff. If you are willing to put in the effort in the very beginning, you will see dividends for years into the future.

I offer solutions and advice for building a network of projects to net you passive income, but I must point out that the most effective way to truly master any avenue is to find a teacher for that specific income source. The material in this book will get you started, but for long term success I suggest you find a teacher for a specific venture that you feel most attached to. This comes from personal experience, as mentors have helped me build my passive income streams over the years.

There is a common misconception about passive income. Many feel that it is income generated by merely doing nothing, that you must find ventures with a minimal investment and simply sit back and enjoy revenue flowing in. The truth is that passive income is more akin to investing – you need to put in up front work to generate long term returns.

In part one of a four part series, you will learn about how to generate passive income through methods that require up front work for long term payoff. In parts one and two of the *Passive Income* series, you will learn the lowest cost methods of building passive income. These are methods of expanding your income streams through investing your time alone. Part one will focus on generating passive income through: eBook writing, YouTube revenue, selling stock photos and licensing audio samples. All of these ventures require little to no investment, as you almost certainly have the equipment to get started with at least some of these projects.

You might have some trepidation about passive income. This is a normal feeling – you are sacrificing labor today for something material in the future. It can be difficult to equate this up front effort for a later payoff; I know this from personal experience. I offer the guidance to get started, the motivation to see the path to profitability, and the advice and strategies you need to start generating a stream of passive income. Continue reading and soon you will have the same enthusiasm that I share for these ventures, understanding the long term pay off and seeing a path forward for your future.

In This Book You Will Find
- An honest and truthful guide for how to build passive income – it requires up front effort, but in return you gain income for long into the future.

- Key strategies for building passive income with little to no investment to get started.
- Considerations for how to get started, the amount of effort required for each venture, and a list of best practices so you can maximize your returns.

Continue reading and soon you will have the starting methods necessary to generate passive income for you and your family. I thought that saving for my future was impossible, and that social security would be my plan for retirement. I want to assure you that passive income is possible for everyone, and that as long as you have the drive, the money will follow. The strategies in the following chapters will require dedication, but what I offer are the secrets and methods to generate additional income streams that will last long into the future. Continue, and soon you will too have this knowledge.

Chapter 1: EBook Writing

The Initial Hump of Self-Doubt

The Internet is the tool of democratizing information in the twenty-first century. Not too long ago the idea of being a publish author was fanciful, and only reserved for those will the greatest talent, and also quite a bit of luck. Today the future is bright for those that wish to supplement their income through writing. A lack of physical publishing allows for this, and eBooks offer a way to make our voice heard through self-publishing. Just like all other forms of passive income in this series, eBook writing is a process that starts slow, but eventually avalanches into building a larger and larger income stream. The amount of revenue that you generate is relative to the total number of eBooks that you sell. This means that while your starting income will be small, as you publish more and more eBooks, this sum will only increase.

EBook writing is a fantastic way to get started with generating passive income. You will need exactly zero dollars to start, and only the gumption to put the effort into writing. I know what many of you readers are thinking right now, 'I can't write, or at least certainly not a whole book'. The phenomenon of digital publishing has allowed for anyone to become a writer, and I don't want you to sell yourself short. The books that you will be writing do not need to be novels, nor will you need to do months of research to create a work that will be beneficial to your readers. The key to eBook writing is two fold: one, you must focus on what the market wants, and two, you must write about topics that you are already intimately familiar with. Having these two attributes in your eBooks will ensure that you are able to generate the income that you desire. You must create books that already have a market, and you must different yourself from other writers by focusing on specific knowledge that only you have. All of this is possible due to the rise of Amazon, and to start the process you must enter this key partnership.

A Partnership with Amazon

Amazon is what makes it possible to generate income through the sale of eBooks. There are other markets for eBooks, and many authors sell works directly to consumers through their own websites. This very well maybe a path for you in the future, but as you are just starting, you will have to work with Amazon. Amazon grants exposure to authors, as well as provides numerous options for setting royalties for their books. Perhaps most importantly, Amazon takes care of processing payments, a huge hurdle for those that wish to sell directly to consumers.

The process of setting up an account to sell eBooks through Amazon is quite simple. Start with going to Amazon Self-Publishing (kdp.azmazon.com). Here, you can log in using your existing account with Amazon. Just a few simple pieces of information are necessary to publish your first book. You will need to supply your tax identification number, your address, and select a number of settings for how you wish to sell your book. I highly recommend that you enroll in the KDP select program, which essentially limits your publishing options to only Kindle for a limited amount of time. As an author that is just starting out, this should be a fine option as your additional avenues for sales are limited. This option also allows you to sell your books to foreign markets, which might turn out to be a sizeable portion of your business. You will need to supply your tax identification number, and this will be used to send a 1099 tax form at the end of the year. Taxes are not the focus of this series, but it is worth noting that you are responsible for paying taxes on any income received through Amazon. One piece of advice for taxes; make sure that you list your total deductions from eBook writing, meaning the cost of the computer that you needed to buy, or any additional expenses.

You will also want to set up your royalty fees, however I suggest that you are conservative in your percentages in the beginning. You will be setting royalties for each country where your books will be sold, but note that this can be done on a book-by-book basis. For payments you will need to attach a checking account or provide an address for where Amazon should mail royalties. You should note that Amazon only pays royalties after you have generated one hundred dollars. This is tied to your account and not individual books. As long as your royalties top one hundred dollars from all of your eBooks, you will be able to cash out. This is a process that builds on top of your past work, so expect to write a few books before you start to receive checks or direct deposits. The great part of this venture is that once you start selling your eBooks, they generally will continue to sell for many months. It is just that first hurdle of creating a work that generates sales, and while it may take some time to get this venture off the ground, it is worth the effort.

Creating an EBook

You may be curious as to the simple mechanics of creating an eBook. Amazon has done a fantastic job of creating tools for authors to sell their material. Form a fantastic web portal based cover creator, to a tool that will convert documents to Kindle format, Amazon offers nearly everything you need to sell an eBook. There are a few details that you will have to work out yourself, as well as some best practices that I highly urge you to stick to.

For starters, the conversion into Kindle format is very straightforward but will require a file converter. Whether you are using Google Docs or Microsoft Word, you will be able to convert to the Kindle format with ease. There is an application on Amazon's Kindle direct website that you must download to make the conversion, and you will also want to download a Kindle reader to ensure that you are formatting your books correctly. The layout of your books is largely up to you, including the font type and number of chapters. I suggest going with a Georgia font (the font used for the book you are reading right now) as it is easy on the eyes, and nearly a standard for eBooks on Amazon. You should also create a clickable table of contents, where each chapter has imbedded hyperlinks. Creating an interactive table of contents is easy, but will require instructions for the specific program that you are using to write your eBook, as it is slightly different across all programs.

There are certain conventions that I urge you to stick to, as they will increase your total number of sales. There are many books on the Amazon Kindle store, and this is your greatest source of competition. While your work might be very important to you, realistically a potentially customer will decide if they find it interesting in a matter of a second or two. Most customers do not decide to read the first chapter (Amazon provides the first few pages free to customers) and then make a purchasing decision. At best they will read the description, and at worst they will look briefly at the cover. It pains me to say, but you will want to pay nearly as much attention to the description and cover for your book as the writing in the book as a whole. The description and cover are your two best marketing tools. Amazon does offer a really great cover creator, but you will want to make sure that your cover is unique in its own right. There are services online to contract artists to create your cover, or you can do it yourself. The description should clearly show what is featured in the book, and ideally have a section with bullet points that sell directly to the customer. I want you to know that you only need to make a few sales to lift a book off the ground – once you start receiving reviews, your book will attract more attention.

You Are an Expert on *Something*

You are now familiar with the mechanics of selling your eBook, but this does little to get you started on *what* you should be writing about. You may be thinking that there is nothing that you are expert on, or that you would find it difficult to write exhaustively about a single topic. To motivate you, I want you to think about this quote: 'Everyone is a snob about something.' There is a lot of truth to this quote, and if you've ever been annoyed by a friend that is deeply obsessed with a single topic, you too know this to be true. There is a topic that is near and dear to your heart, and it is likely that since you feel relatively alone in your enthusiasm, you believe that no one wishes to hear your thoughts – this cannot be further from the truth. Whether your passion is cars, speakers, video games, cinema or painting, we all have a topic that we care deeply about, and there are others that share this enthusiasm.

I suggest that you write your first eBook on a topic that you deeply care about. What's important is that you are specific as possible when writing about a topic. If you care a lot about cars, write about something more specific, like cars from a certain era, or cars from a certain country. If you love video games, this too can be made more specific by focusing on a niche topic within the greater category of video games. It is likely that your first book is not going to sell many copies, and in fact it is likely to not sell any copies at first. The reason why you first want to focus on a niche topic that you care about is because it gives you the extra motivation to get to work and create an eBook. The initial effort that goes into writing is going to be your greatest hurdle as you get started. Anything you can do to improve your enjoyment of this work is very beneficial. After you have created your first eBook, it becomes rather easy to convince yourself to write more. It is just that initial hump that you have to get over.

Your path forward with eBooks, and how you will eventually get sales from your first book, is going to be based on your total output and linking to your other works. Suppose that one of your later books becomes quite popular – for starters this will have an immediate boom on your old works, simply because clicking on the author page will link to your other books. To improve the attachment rate to your older books, you should also link to your other material. Books don't necessarily need to all be on one topic to link to each other, as what book readers want is a particular style of writing. Disparate topics are fine as long as you infuse enough of your personality into your writing. Your readership will appreciate this and it will be a driver of sales of your other material.

Focus on Demand

While your starting books should be works of passion, you should also focus on some topics that are in demand on Amazon. Take a look at the top sellers on Amazon Kindle, and scroll through the results until you start to see authors and books that you don't recognize. The best of the top sellers are going to be digital versions of popular authors' works, but results of around fifty and above start to get into the territory of eBook writers. Many of the popular topics on Amazon are finance books, and while this is very technical niche, there are additional topics that might be intriguing to you. While I personally do not have any material out on the topic, I believe that anything on Donald Trump is likely to at least catch the eye of readers. This may not be a trending topic among lesser known eBook writers, but it is only a matter of time until someone breaks through with a great book.

Focusing on topics that are in demand is a great way to bring attention to your niche specific books. Writing on these hot topics is going to be a little bit more difficult, as it is likely that you do not always have the require knowledge to fill out an entire book. This may require some research on your part, but you should have the motivation to complete a book after you have written about your passion topic. Truly, it is not that difficult to write an eBook; you just have to prove it to yourself that you have it within you to write. That being said, if you truly find it a difficult process to write, there is an alterative avenue you can take, but it requires an up front monetary investment.

Ghostwriting Services

When creating eBooks that are not on a topic that you are highly passionate about, you can hire ghostwriters to write material for you. There are a number of services online, ranging from freelance writers on UpWork.com, to companies that specialize in ghostwriting services. To create material this way, you will need to be very specific in the instructions that you provide to a writer. While they will be filling in the book, it is up to you to create a guide for the material that should be covered – the more specific the better the quality of the eBook.

Lastly, while you will not have to write these books yourself, there is an upfront cost to paying ghostwriters. There are many options available to you at many different price points. It is my suggestion that you do not use a writer that accepts less than one dollar per one hundred words. There are many freelance writers on UpWork that will write for far less than this, but realistically these are not native English speakers. I have seen this type of writing on Amazon before, mainly when looking at the competition, and seeing what books are in demand. You need to make sure that you are paying enough that you get a quality that is consistent with a native English speaker, and that you have someone that can fulfill your outline.

Volume and Time Frame

The amount of passive income generated through eBook sales is relative to the number of total number of eBooks that you have published. You should expect that this a six-month endeavor before you start to generate true income through eBook sales. I mention this because I have seen complaints about eBooks not generating sales immediately – it's a crowded marketplace and you need some time for your material to make it into the hands of readers. Just like any other type of investment, you have to be forward thinking and look to the future. Don't worry if your books don't take off immediately; just put your head down, create the material, and wait for the benefits to pay off in a few months time.

Grammar, Style and Common Concerns

I realize that many of you readers may think that you do not have what it takes to write. I'm not talking about creating content, or a lack of ideas, but simply that your current job does not require writing and you haven't practiced long form writing in a number of years. I certainly started this way, realizing that I truly hadn't written large works since college. EBook writing is far different than academic writing – it is an entirely different beast. The books that you write need to flow well; the sentence structure needs to *read* correctly, but this does not necessarily mean that the grammar needs to be perfect. This is not an assignment that is to be graded. This is reading for pleasure and so as long as your writing voice is conversational and flows well, you will do fine. This does not mean that your grammar can be terrible, and spelling mistakes rampant, but it does mean that if you have large concerns about the quality of your writing, you should remember the ultimate purpose; you are writing books for entertainment, not for academia. Make sure that the flow is correct, and that the material is interesting. Grammar is important, but don't let it bog you down – it's a concern, but not the gravest one.

A Quick Note on Fiction Writing

I mentioned that you need to write about a topic that you care deeply about, a topic that have some passion fore. It is important that what you write veers more towards educational rather than fiction. It is a simple truth that fiction writers on Amazon simply do not sell that many copies of their books. Writing fiction is something that a lot of people do merely as a hobby, and Amazon has not provided an outlet for them to sell their material. There are compilations of science fiction stories, romantic novels, realistic fiction, and every imaginable topic you can think of; nearly none of it sells as well as educational material. That being said, the fiction books that *do* sell are some of the best selling eBooks on Amazon. The key is that a writer needs to hit a critical mass of readers before they find great success. Also, these books tend to take longer to create, and also the pricing on fiction is typically less than on educational books.

It is entirely your decision if you want to focus on writing fiction, but know that it will be altogether a much more difficult process to make any real money. You will need to create longer material, and sell it for less money. You will face greater competition, and you will need to make sure that the topic you write about is very specific. If you want to write science fiction, make it a niche topic within science fiction, such as time travel. The reason for you need to get specific within a topic is simply because of the way that the Amazon search system works. You will want to put your fiction material into niche genres so that it can more easily be searched. Lastly, with fiction writing there is a greater sense of ownership of the material, or at least this is what I have found among the writers I know. When one educational book does not sell, it is understandable to the author, but when their fiction book doesn't sell, it often feels like a personal insult. The competition is steep and these feelings shouldn't percolate, but they often do and it is all the more reason to focus on niche educational material.

Chapter 2: YouTube Ad Revenue

Requirements

EBooks have zero cost to entry and require only the most basic of equipment. Making money through ad revenue on YouTube is an entirely different proposition, and will require more equipment. Most readers of this book will already have a laptop with a webcam, but there are some additional considerations to take into account. For one, there is the simple issue of bandwidth and upload speed. Internet packages typically differentiate the upload and download speeds within each package, with the download speed almost always being far greater than the upload. Unfortunately, to put videos on YouTube you are going to need a decent upload speed. By going to SpeedTest.net, you can determine your upload and download speed. At a bare minimum, you will need a 1mbs upload connection, with 5-30 being far more preferable. A 1mbs upload will take around eight hours for a single twenty minute video running at a high bit rate (quality of video compression). Additionally, when you upload a video to YouTube, there is a high amount of compression done on YouTube's servers, so you will want to upload the highest quality raw video. Put simply, anything you upload to YouTube is going to look far worse than it does locally on your machine.

Aside from bandwidth, you will need a camera that is preferably 720p or greater and an editing/recording program. If

18

you are running MacOS, the built in iMovie is a great starter program, with easy instructions and simple to use editing tools. If you are running Windows, I would defer to either Sony Vegas or Adobe Movie Maker. Sony Vegas is more advanced, and the licensing can be quite expensive. Unfortunately on Windows, these are the two best options, but for beginners neither is quite as easy to use as iMovie. These programs are essential to uploading videos because this is where you will determine the output render of your video – meaning this is where you will determine the bitrate and resolution of your project.

If the requirements seem a bit technical, and perhaps even scary, do not fret. Uploading videos is easy; you will just need a fair amount of practice. Expect to really get a handle on video editing and uploading after around ten to twenty hours of practice. It's an investment for sure, but successful YouTube videos are some of the greatest ways of providing passive income. Note that most YouTube personalities do have a second job, and that it does take quite a bit of time to build a following large enough to quit your day job. I would plan on using YouTube videos to merely supplement your income. Making YouTube your full time job is an admirable goal, but realistically your revenue will be more limited.

Revenue

Uploading videos to YouTube and getting views won't make you any income on its own right – you will need to link your account to AdSense to make any revenue. This is a simple process and requires going through the AdSense portal, but note that once you sign up for AdSense, you are held to additional terms and conditions. The only negative aspect of this is that copyright infringement, which is often done accidently, can either lead to your video being taken down or your revenue being held by Google.

The breakdown of revenue from AdSense is 55% for the creator and 45% for Google. Just like with eBooks, you will need to make one hundred dollars or more to receive payment. Also, you will need to supply your tax identification number and declare any payments as income. Just like eBooks, if you buy any equipment to fulfill this project, make sure you add that to your deductions. In terms of potential profit, video creators earn around $7 per every one thousand views. While this might seem like a small amount, three videos a month that garner 4,000 views each would equal over one thousand dollars a year. Just like eBooks, this is also a process that builds on top of your past efforts. As you build an audience and gain subscribers you will find that your attachment rate to videos increases, so your past videos will earn views and that audience will be with you going forward.

Personality or Utility

You have a general sense of the requirements for uploading your videos, as well as how you will be generating revenue. The most important aspect of your YouTube channel is going to be building a community and creating niche specific content for your audience. The most successful YouTubers typically split into one of two categories, utility or personality. Utility videos are designed with a purpose of teaching a skill or helping an audience deal with a problem. Consider videos that show car repair, or instructional videos as utility. The other type of YouTube channel is personality driven. While these videos do offer some aspect of educational material to their viewers, most are there because of the personality behind the channel. How you want to designate yourself is largely going to depend on how outgoing you are. If you find yourself to really be a shy person, I suggest that create utility videos on a topic you are familiar with – it's generally less profitable, but it plays to the idea that you want to be known for the utility of your content, and not your personality. If you are an outgoing person, YouTube is a fantastic venue to get your personality on the screens of potentially millions of viewers. Decide on the angle that you want to approach your YouTube channel with, and focus on being as niche as possible. Even if you are mainly selling your personality, you will need a general topic to lure in viewers. Some of the most popular topics are: video games, makeup, product reviews, and comedy channels. All of these are good avenues if you want to create a following using your personality. The videos will revolve around you, but you will get those initial views through these popular search terms.

Consistency

Uploading YouTube videos can certainly be a lot of work, especially depending on the quality of the editing. What is important is that you are consistent in your uploads. Whether that means a video every day, every week, or every month, make sure that your audience knows when they can expect new content. I've seen more YouTube channels die this way than for any other reason - the creator is simply not consistent enough in their uploads and their audience peters off. I like to equate this to the *Lost* problem. *Lost* was a popular show on ABC, but started to decline in ratings when they became highly inconsistent in when it would air. Viewers need a sense of community and a sense of consistency to revisit your channel over and over.

Building a Community

A few years ago Amazon bought Twitch.TV for around a billion dollars. I remember this acquisition and being quite puzzled. I didn't realize that Twitch was such a popular service, and didn't understand how it was different from YouTube. The secret to building a strong viewership on YouTube is to build a community. Your viewers are not just there to see you – they are there to interact with like-minded individuals. Twitch is the epitome of building a community around videos, and what differentiates it is the 'live' element to its videos. Twitch and YouTube play into each other, and depending on the topic you want to focus on, I suggest you take a look at using both services.

Twitch is actually easier to use than YouTube in a lot of cases as you do not need to focus on video editing or uploading a large amount of data at one time. Open Broadcast Software (OBS) has made streaming an incredibly simple process, and truly it is easier than getting started on YouTube. These two communities should play into each other in the sense that you use the live streaming of Twitch to link back to your YouTube channel. What Twitch offers is a live chat function so that you can interact with your audience. While many Twitch streamers use this to play video games and communicate at the same time, there are many other potential uses. Regardless of what your niche topic is, you can use live streaming to great effect. Take for instance if you decide to focus on reviews of makeup products, a popular type of video category. YouTube videos are not interactive, but Twitch allows you to answer questions live. Perhaps most importantly, it is a very simple process to download videos from Twitch and then upload them to YouTube. If you are unsure about using video editing software, this is a great way to start uploading videos. You do not need to worry about encoding, bitrate or any other settings. You will set these options up through OBS, and even this has an automatic detection system that works fairly well. I have thus far not mentioned that YouTube also has a live streaming service, but unlike Twitch it appears to not be very popular. If you want to focus on a live aspect, I highly recommend using Twitch over

YouTube – the videos will still make their way to YouTube, but they just won't be streamed live on that service.

There are several ways of interacting with your community to draw greater viewership. One of the most common ways is through giving away a product to one of your viewers. This works better on Twitch since it is a live system, but it also commonly done on YouTube. Remember that even if your giveaway is on Twitch, this will still play into YouTube views as long as your Twitch channel redirects to your YouTube page. There are also many plugins that you can attach to the Twitch chat for greater interaction, such as polls and competition among users. One of the more inventive methods that I have seen is using a video game to interact with a large audience. Streamers have used a modern version of *You Don't Know Jack* to interact with thousands of viewers live. This is a fantastic way to further your reach and to gain views.

While your main monetization is through YouTube, if you decide to also stream through Twitch, you can make revenue through this site as well. Instead of going through AdSense, you can set up a Patreon account. You can think of this as a tip jar for your efforts. Again, it's not going to be your main driver of revenue from videos, but is just a nice way to make some additional income for your steaming efforts.

Marketing

There are a number of ways to market your videos outside of YouTube and Twitch. Look to popular content sites like Reddit for an avenue to link your videos. You can also find success by linking relevant videos in Yahoo comments, or other popular online forums. The key is that you are convincing when you link videos, and do not come off as a bot that posts a link on every single comment thread. Apply the links only when relevant, and be conservative in how often you post.

Within YouTube, you can link to videos using the simple to use overlay system. This system puts links to your other videos on top of the video that is currently playing. You should have at least one link to another video and one to subscribe to your channel. This is a staple of self-promotion on YouTube, but some YouTubers go about this method in a way that is entirely too forceful. I've seen many videos that get covered in overlay ads, to the point that it detracts from the experience of watching the video. Like with comments, be conservative in your overlay links. Remember that you are trying to generate passive income through hard work and investment in the immediate – you should not be treating YouTube as a way of paying your bills in the next month, so please do not try and seem too desperate within your channel.

Niche Topics and Answering a Question

The best way to differentiate yourself from other YouTubers is to get highly specific about a topic. You may think that this does not serve the purpose of mainstream appeal, but keep in mind how crowded this marketplace is. The ability to upload YouTube videos is in the hands of nearly everyone, and

25

so focusing first on niche topics is a great way to find your footing. You are also marketing your personality, and niche channels will often grow based on how much your audience enjoys your company. Additionally, even the most niche topic is going to have thousands or millions of people that are interested. YouTube is available to billions of people across the globe, so even just a slice of a small market can lead to thousands of views every month.

As you create your videos, I want you to focus on answering a question in every video that you create. This is a strategy that many YouTube personalities have adopted – solve a problem or answer a question for your audience. The question or problem needs to be provided by you, and what this does is build a through line for your videos. They will have a beginning, middle and end in addressing whatever question you pose. Obviously this does not work as well with humor, but that is entirely different beast from most YouTube videos. A question focuses your video, but also offers a reward to the viewer – they will understand a topic or be able to solve a problem that they previously could not address. This gives purpose to your channel, and will attract viewers. This is merely a beginning tactic, and helps you outline the structure of your videos. The question that you try and answer does not need to be incredibly specific, but can be quite broad, such as: what is a good coffee bean from South America? In this question we do not have a hyper specific problem that we are trying to solve, but rather a general topic of inquiry. It focuses the video to a single topic, and helps you outline the direction of your content.

Production Quality

The long term success of your YouTube channel is dependent on many variables, but one you cannot discount is the overall quality of the production. Even if go the route of streaming to Twitch and then uploading these videos to YouTube, you will need to make sure that the raw video feed is high enough quality to keep viewers glued to your channel. For example, even if you have a truly great niche topic, and even if you are a fantastic teacher, if the audio crackles or the resolution of your video is not fantastic, viewers will go elsewhere. No matter how specific a topic you discuss, there are going to be other YouTubers that also focus on that material. Your videos might have better content but viewers won't get that far into your videos if the quality is not great.

This is a perfect aspect to look for a mentor to help you. You know the basic software that you should use, as well as some of the technical requirements, but like all aspects of passive income, there are many details that I am skimming over. In this case, specifically the technical side of achieving great uploads. I suggest you find a video series on YouTube that deals with this issue specifically. Specific channels can guide you through the type of bitrate that is best, as well as how to use video editing software to its greatest effect. It's fine if your starting videos are a little rough around the edges as everyone starts this way, but to find long term success you are going to meet a certain level of quality that viewers have come to expect.

Be Mindful of Copyright Infringement

There is a bit of a crisis in the YouTube community, and that is how the current copyright system for videos works. Even without AdSense, if your video uses copyrighted music without permission, it might be taken down. The moment you turn AdSense on, this gets exponentially more stringent. There are firms dedicated to issuing take down notices and many YouTubers have to face a reality that their videos can be taken down at any time. Even worse, Google holds the revenue from that video until it has reviewed the complaint. In essence, those that own the copyrighted material have a great amount of authority over what videos stay up. They do not need to prove infringement to get a video suspended, and while this system might be unfair, YouTube is such a large market that these are the rules you will have to abide to.

The best way then to avoid take down notices is to not put any licensed music in your videos. You can put your own created music in videos, but note that even this carries a chance of being taken down– truly the system is biased to copyright holders. If they feel as though a piece of music you created borrows from a song that they own the right to, even if it is by accident, they will issue a complaint.

Take down notices are an issue for every YouTubers, but it is especially prevalent in the video game community. Some modern games include a specific streaming option that allows for copyrighted music to be turned off, but many do not have this option. This means that if you are playing *Grand Theft Auto* for example, and a song by a popular artist comes on, your whole video can be taken down. Additionally, there are some publishers and product creators that want a cut of revenue from showing their products. Nintendo, for example, requires an agreement that they receive a large portion of your revenue. There are other manufacturers of goods that will do the same, issuing a complaint until you agree to enter a contract where they receive a portion of your revenue. Be mindful of these companies, and be weary of the music that you include in your videos.

It can be frustrating to have your videos taken down when you do not understand the nature of a complaint against you. I want to offer some reassurance that not all take down notices are permanent, and many are lifted after review. Also the more subscribers you garner, the faster your review will take place. This is important if you are dealing with time sensitive videos, such as a review of weekly events, or a review for a product that has just been released. If revenue is being held because of a copyright complaint, this too will be paid to you if Google decides that no infringement has taken place.

Lastly, I should mention that many infringement complaints come from other YouTubers that compete in the same market. YouTube is a highly competitive marketplace, and there are some less than honest video creators. They will claim that your video infringes on theirs, and since the current system favors those that issue complaints, the video will cease to earn ad revenue until it has been under review. This is yet another reason why it is highly advisable that you focus on a niche specific market. The less competition that you face, the lower the chance your video will be taken down.

Chapter 3: Stock Photos

Profit Through Artistry

Whether you're an aspiring photographer, or merely enjoy doing it for fun, there is an opportunity to make passive income through selling your photos to companies that host stock images. Stock images are generic photos that can be used for many different purposes. From online articles, to eBook covers, stock photos are used by many different websites looking for photos to attach to their content. Some of the larger companies that sell stock photos online are ShutterStock and iStockPhoto. For example, in chapter one you learned about how you can generate income through writing eBooks. In generating this material you will want to have a high quality cover, and stock photos often are a perfect fit for many online writers. There are stock photos for just about every topic you can imagine, and often times photos are sold merely because they emphasize a specific emotion or aspect to a business that needs to be accentuated.

The quality of stock images needs to be high, at least in a technical sense. You will want to have images that are at least 2560 by 1440, or 1440p resolution. Your camera will likely capture photos at a much higher resolution, but this is the minimum resolution you should use on your uploaded photos. Often the highest resolution photo is not the one used as a stock image, but the higher the quality of the original photo, the more likely that photo is going to sell on stock photo websites. Do not worry about creating multiple versions of your pictures at different resolution, or creating a watermark background to prevent infringement – these details are left to the stock photo websites.

There are essentially no parameters for the type of photos that you can take, so feel free to snap shots of nature, cities or any uncopyrighted material. You will want to keep in mind that subjects in your photos may need to be compensated for their effort. It is for this reason that I suggest you use yourself or family members, and maybe even friends as subjects. Be sure that you are up front with exactly what you are trying to accomplish, and let the person you are shooting know that they will be featured in a stock image. You should also clarify that these photos can end up *anywhere*. They may be used to promote a business that you find attractive, or they could be used for less appealing cases, like an endorsement for a medicine to a horrible medical condition – the implication being that the subject in the photo has the medical condition in question.

As you start, focus on taking photos that truly *only you* can take. If you live in Nevada for example, focus on shots of the landscape and conditions that cannot be captured in any other part of the United States. This helps differentiate your photos from the competition. This is also a quest for a high volume of photos. Each picture will need to be distinct from one another, but you will need to collect a large amount of photos to find any true profitability. The amount of money that you collect per photo is relatively small, so take as many picture as possible. Do note that like all other projects in this series, selling stock photos is a process that builds on top of your past efforts. Your sales will avalanche over time, but expect a small volume of sales as you are just getting started.

Driving Sales

There is a key question in what type of photos drive the most sales. Put simply, think about how stock photos are found – clients search for photos with large overarching terms, like 'trees', 'nature' and 'business'. This is hardly specific, but can be used to your advantage. Depending on the site that you license your photos to, you may have the opportunity to tag your photos and collate them into albums. Try and create your albums with these large overarching searches in mind. It pains me to say this, but my research has shown that some of the best selling images are in fact the most generic ones. The more specific the subject, the fewer clients you are likely to attract. Since this is a numbers game, you will want to take pictures with the greatest market appeal.

You can start by focusing on your key advantage of being in a location that other photographers simply are not. Start with photos that take advantage of your specific geographic region, and create albums based around seasons, and the subjects of large search terms. Whether those subjects are rock formations, trees or animals, you will fair far better if your albums stick to a single topic at hand. The reasoning for this is quite simple – as clients look through your photos they will tend to make that initial click on your material based on a particular subject. The more photos that you have of that subject, the greater chance of licensing your photos.

Consider Site Exclusivity

There are a number of places to sell your stock photos, and there are essentially two mainline strategies to drive revenue. You can either sell your photos to multiple outlets, or you can sign an exclusive deal with one website. For example iStockphoto will pay around three times the standard rate if you do not license your photos to any other website. The math behind making the most profit is not as clear as it might seem however, as currently the market leader in selling stock photos does not have such a large market share to make this the most logical choice.

For myself, I found that through experimentation it is more profitable to license your photos to as many websites as possible. This has to do with the competing marketplace for stock photos, as sales and other incentives have made for a diverse marketplace where there is no clear market leader. iStockphoto may generate more sales during part of the year, but their competitors will adjust rates to drive and peel off customers. Still, this is a question that you may want to save for your mentor if you decide to reach one, as they will have more specific advice for how to license your photos.

Receiving Payment

Just like with Amazon and Google, you will need to make a certain amount of revenue before a website will pay out on your material. This is one of the considerations for selling photos to a single website, as it is more likely that you will earn the base payout amount due to the greater fees. If you are looking for more immediate income, this may be your best route to profitability. If you are looking for longer term revenue, I would license your photos to multiple sites. The payout benchmarks tend to be around $50 to $100, and just like other services you will need to provide your tax identification number and declare any profit as income on your tax returns.

Post Processing

The raw images you shoot are the main driver of revenue, but you cannot discount using post processing software to enhance your images. There is a level of artistry needed to manipulate your photos in editing software, and I have found that often artists will overdo the level of effects to the point that the raw image is somewhat ruined. Consider using Adobe Photoshop or Premier to enhance your photos or to create something that cannot be captured in reality. These photos tend to do quite well as it is an additional technical skill that many photographers do not have. Some of the types of manipulations you can focus on are creating merges of multiple seasons into a single photo, or shooting something that breaks the law of physics, like a subject hovering over the ground. What's neat about this particular avenue is that depending on how much you manipulate your photos, you may end up with multiple samples all from the same initial photograph. It is worth mentioning that this can be a time intensive process, and you will need the proper software license and technical skills to manipulate photos.

Considerations

With eBook writing and creating YouTube videos, it is likely that you already have all of the resources needed to create content. Looking at photography, we start to get into an area where the odds of needed investment are much higher. You cannot take photos using your smartphone, no matter how many megapixels your camera has. It is true that smartphone cameras have gotten quite advanced over the years, but your competition online is going to have more professional equipment. This does not mean that you need to spend several hundred dollars on an expensive camera, but it does mean you may want to spend around $100 to $200 on a point and shoot camera of modest quality – even these will shoot better photos than most smart phones. This up front cost should be a main consideration, and if you are unsure of about pursing this avenue, take the time to weigh your options and decide if you want this to be one of your potential income streams.

The ever increasing competition in stock photos has meant that a lot of photographers will differentiate themselves with expensive pieces of equipment. In the last few years this has manifest in aerial shots using drones. Drones are expensive pieces of equipment that require a high level of skill to use. I do not advise that you run out and buy a drone to get a leg up on the competition, but it should be a consideration down the line, particularly if you are already interested in drone photography.

Additionally there is the question of natural talent when it comes to photography. Unlike many other arts, I feel as though the skill required to take great photos is vastly understated. You will need a certain eye for photos – not necessarily to take the most beautiful shots, but to know what customers will be interested in. To get started I suggest that you take a look at several stock photo websites and explore some of the more popular shots in categories that you are most likely to focus on. For example if you plan on taking shots of nature, look for pictures in your specific biome and see the level of artistry and style that you are competing with. These photos will give you an idea as to what you are trying to capture, and as you start it is advisable that you focus on imitation, trying to create similar pieces of art by using established stock image photographers for reference material.

Chapter 4: Selling Audio Tracks

Profit Without Recognition

Selling audio samples is a great way to generate passive income, even if you aren't necessarily a musician. There are a number of sites where you can sell audio samples of all types, ranging from sound effects manufactured to noises captured in nature. This is a highly competitive market, and unlike stock photos, it is relatively difficult to look at a wide variety of samples at one time. A client needs to actually listen to each track to decide if they want it and this takes time.

There are two main avenues of selling audio tracks. You can either license music and loops, or you can sell specific audio samples. Either avenue will require some specific equipment, and this is a route best taken if you have some experience working with audio software. In terms of generating loops or beats, you can use software like Fruity-Loops and Garage Band (bundled with MacOS computers) to generate music. These tracks do not need to be particularly long, nor do they need to be entirely complete. You are selling part of a song that will be put together at a later time and in addition to your base audio sample, there will be many layers put on top of your initial efforts. This means that while what you need to generate is catchy and appealing, it does not need to be a finished work on its own. The second method is to create sound effects using very short samples, somewhere around three to five second. Samples are sounds like glass breaking or the sound of a rock hitting the floor. This second route might sound much more simple, but the truth is that it will require just as much, if not more effort.

Making decent money through selling complete songs is a difficult prospect in 2017, and I suggest that you avoid trying to license complete works. Finished songs can be licensed through Pandora and Spotify, but even getting onto these services is not the most simple processes. Additionally, the number of listeners for your audio tracks that you need to acquire is immense before you can receive any type of profit. I know this through experience, as creating music has been a hobby of mine for years. It is easier than ever to put yourself on the Internet, but the competition has never been steeper. There is also a perception in the marketplace that music simply isn't worth anything - songs aren't paid for, they are streamed and the only payment are the advertisements through Spotify and other streaming services. If you want to make complete musical works, I suggest that you focus these efforts through YouTube as music nowadays is a complete product. It needs to be sold with an image and a personality behind the music, as the pure merit of great songs hardly ever generates sales on its own. There are exceptions to be sure, but for a vast majority of artists, they need to be *seen* in addition to being heard to build an audience.

Equipment and Additional Considerations

Selling audio samples is the most expensive venture in part one of this series, particularly if you are selling short sound effects. You will need both the right software and equipment to generate the sounds that you want. Often a single recording is not enough to sell a sample, and instead you will need to layer sounds to get a specific three to five second sample. Take for instance all of the sounds that go into a manufactured 'punch', or the sound of flesh hitting flesh. This is a needed effect in many movies, and recording an actual punch almost never generates the desired sound. Instead, it is a combination of sounds layered on top of each other to get the feeling of a fist connecting with flesh. Additionally, often times the way that these sounds are layered do not make the most intuitive sense. A punch might be combination of hammer hitting a cow carcass, combined with a rock hitting the ground. This might sound extremely strange, but truly this is how audio samples are generated. Doing this on your own requires the software and the skill. While I would define myself as musically inclined, I cannot say that selling sound effects has been a large boom for myself – it requires a special set of skills that I fear I simply do not have. I mention it as an option because it is specialized skill that can generate great passive income, but only if you have what it takes to manufacture these effects.

When it comes to making audio loops and samples, this is far lower cost to entry. You do not need to own musical instruments or have any fancy recording equipment to make beats. You really only need the software, and there are so many competing companies that he raw cost to entry is very low. Garage Band for Mac is a free program that is quite fully featured and can be used to create high quality beats. Fruity Loops requires a license, but even this is moderately priced. I also want to say that you do not need to have innate musical skill to create high quality beats. This might sound ridiculous on its face, but often great work can be done merely through experimentation. When the input device is a computer keyboard, it is simply a matter of arranging the notes through the software and finding beats that you enjoy. You can sell these on any number of sites, with some of the most popular being LoopSeekers.com, ProducerLooops, and SoundClick. What is unique about selling audio loops is that many websites allow you to price them how you would like, so you can sell your samples for what you deem to be the appropriate price. This is important because it is an additional way to differentiate yourself from the competition – you can lower your price to drive more sales.

As with other methods of generating passive income in this series, you will need to provide your tax identification number to licensing sites. Additionally the more samples that you sell, and the more time that each sample is listed, the more revenue you will gain. Start with just a few samples and the initial returns will be low, but over time and as you build your collection, this will increase until it is a healthy stream of income.

Conclusion

Thank you again for downloading *Passive Income: Part One*.

You now have the base knowledge to start earning passive income through four methods that require as little zero dollars to start. While each method does have specific requirements, you should find that these avenues of generating passive income are widely accessible. Keep in mind that each strategy listed will take a number of months to pay off, but when royalties start to come in, they tend to flow for many months, or even years. It is getting over that initial hump of convincing yourself to make the effort to generate content for rewards at a later time – if you can do this, you can find long term success.

The most important aspect about passive income is to understand the idea of initial upfront work. I have seen many eBooks that claim you can earn passive income without lifting a finger – this is truly fanciful. It takes that initial effort, that initial sweat and dedication to earn money for long into the future. There is a reason why so many Americans do not try these avenues of investment, and that is because it takes that work ethic and effort to get these ventures off the ground. By merely being familiar with the four ways of earning passive income discussed in this book, you already have a leg up on the competition. Build the dedication and find the motivation to start investing your time now for revenue later and I'm sure that you will find success for your efforts.

If you enjoyed the material discussed in this book, and are looking for additional ways to earn passive income, please consider looking at the other books in this series. Later books will detail additional methods of making income, and will focus on investments of both time, and a little bit of money. Passive income is a process that builds on top of itself – the more income streams that you can get off the ground, the more profit you can generate for you and your family. Please find links to the other books in this series below the conclusion.

Lastly if you enjoyed this book, it would be much appreciated if you could leave a review on Amazon. The best way for this book to make its way into the hands of more readers is through truthful reviews about this work. Please write what you liked about this book and what could be improved upon. Any and all feedback is helpful as I continue to serve the needs of my readership.

Thank you and good luck.

Passive Income

Incredible Ideas of How to Make Money While You Sleep

Part Two

Passive Income Series

Part One:
    EBook Writing
    YouTube Ad Revenue
    Stock Photos
    Audio Samples

Part Two:
    Print per Demand
    Instagram
    Creating Online Courses

Part Three:
    P2P Lending
    Creating Apps
    Joint Venture Partnerships

Part Four:
    Selling Your Product or Service
    Affiliate Marketing
    Dividend Stocks

Introduction

I want to thank you and congratulate you for downloading *Passive Income: Part Two*.

Welcome to part two of a four part series on generating passive income. Parts one and two of this series focus on generating passive income with the smallest possible investment. In part one I discussed how to generate revenue streams through EBook writing, YouTube ad revenue, and selling stock images and audio samples. In part two, we will continue to focus on generating passive income through the smallest possible monetary investment. This does not mean that there will be no labor involved, but simply that you will not need a large sum of money to get started. These are projects that are time intensive, and also are connected to one another. I highly suggest that if you have not read part one that you start there before continuing onto part two. Note that parts three and four will focus on additional passive income techniques, but these will rely on a strong monetary investment with a smaller time commitment.

There is a strong misconception about passive income, that money can be generated by merely doing nothing other than a modest investment. This cannot be further from the truth, and anyone that tries to sell you this idea is merely offering you snake oil. Passive income is a function of two inputs: time and money. I know that for many American households, either input may be difficult to come by for generating income. What I offer are strategies, tips, and avenues of investment for supplementing your income. These are realistic ventures that you can adopt, and while the initial sum that you generate will be small, passive income is like any other investment in that it builds on top of your past efforts. As you expand you reach and work on more ventures, you will find your supplemental income grow larger and larger. Passive income is up front investment for long term payoff – put in the work now and you will see dividends for long in the future.

All of the material in this series is meant to give you a brief overview, along with considerations and strategies for getting started. You will know the type of investment required, whether that is time or money. To truly master any *single* venture, you should note that a mentor is the best way to fine tune your skills.

As we continue into part two, this book will focus on generating income from low monetary investment ventures. All of these ventures will require a decent amount of your time, but this should be a signal to you that these are ventures that will eventually generate profit. Something truly easy would be adopted by everyone – you must look for avenues of income that require hard work, as these are genuine profit makers. Continue and you will learn how to generate passive income through creating a print per demand business, attracting marketers through Instagram, and creating your own online courses to spread your specialized knowledge. If you enjoy the material in this book, I suggest that you pick up the additional books in this series, listed below the conclusion.

In This Book You Will Find

- An honest and truthful guide for how to build passive income – it requires up front effort, but in return you gain income for long into the future.
- Key strategies for building passive income with little to no investment to get started.
- Considerations for how to get started, the amount of effort required for each venture, and a list of best practices so you can maximize your returns.

Chapter 5: Print per Demand

What is Print per Demand?

In late 2016, I was at a friend's home playing a game on their television. It was a form of *You Don't Know Jack*, where each player participated by entering answers through their smart phones. There was one mini-game that struck me as the epitome of print per demand in 2016-17. The game was built around designing a t-shirt using simple shapes on your smartphone. The winner of the game was the person whose t-shirt won the most votes from the participants of the game. It seemed a bit silly at the time, and it wasn't clear why we were creating designs for t-shirts. Seemingly the designs could have been for posters, or could be abstracted to a digital canvas. It wasn't until the end of the game that it became clear – for $15 you could order any one of the t-shirts created and they would be shipped right to your door. This, in essence, is print per demand.

A company will make any number of an item per demand, whether that is a single item or a thousand. This may seem like a minor technological breakthrough, but if you remember what it used to take to make a t-shirt, this is quite extraordinary. Before print per demand, you would have to be concerned about economics of scale – it often only made sense to print many t-shirts because to print a single one would be far too expensive. Today we can print a single book, a single t-shirt, a single poster, and the cost per item is low enough that we can find profit even through small orders.

To make a passive income stream through print per demand, you must focus on creating items that are in demand. This is an avenue of making profit by getting out into your local town and city and working with established businesses, bands, community centers and other organizations to supply them with all sorts of print per demand items. If you read book one in this series, you might also be seeing the implication for printing your eBooks and selling physical copies. Expressed in the first book, this is a service that Amazon offers for all of their eBooks, but there are additional ways in which you can print your finished books and sell them locally.

The key to making a strong revenue stream through print per demand is to create either attractive pieces of art, or material for utility, like eBooks. If you find yourself to not be much of an artist, that should actually be of little concern. There is no reason for you to be making all of the logos and designs that will be printed – you can in fact license images from artists online. I look to DeviantArt.com as one of the main outlets for finding great designs that cost a relatively small fee to license. These are artists that are just staring out, and since they are not established they will take a reduced licensing fee merely to get exposure. Your role and economic utility is in providing the printing services and getting exposure for these lesser known artists. In this situation, everyone wins and everyone is serving their own purpose for the greater ideal of getting product into the hands of consumers.

There is of course another avenue, and one that is more profitable, creating your own designs and logos for t-shirts and posters. This is a particular skill that I do not have, and I mostly license the images that I use. You can bypass the licensing fees by making the designs yourself, but note that I have found one main issue concerning selling your own art – you are judging it based on your own perspective. For example, when you license an image from an artist, you are using your artistic eye to see that it would be a demanded product. It is much harder to be objective when looking at your own art. It's just a matter of fact that artists often have trouble distinguishing their best works from their mediocre ones. There is a chance that you will try and sell the 'wrong' designs. They might be the ones that you like, but they might not be the ones that move printed products. This is just a consideration and does not mean that you shouldn't make your own logos and designs. If anything, I would merely suggest that you have a loved one or friend go over the designs with you, so that you have a second opinion on what would popular. You should also note that it is unlikely that you will be credited with any of the designs and logos you create. This is true for both licensed images (unless the artist requires their signature on the print) and your own. I have read extensively about the printing business, and this seems to be an issue that irks some artists. If you don't particularly mind, that's just fine, but you should just note that you likely won't be finding recognition through printing.

I am going to emphasize selling your printed products in person, or at least negotiating deals with resellers in person, but you should also be selling your material online. I would advise setting up an Amazon marketplace account where you are essentially a subsidiary of the greater Amazon store. Orders will come through Amazon to you, and you will mail product to customers. There is truly only one drawback to an online store, and that is the delay between ordering a t-shirt from your supplier and then shipping it to a customer. You will want to have some inventory in your home or wherever you are shipping product from. This way you can fulfill orders as fast as possible. Otherwise, you are looking at up to a two week delay to get your orders through to customers. For my own purposes, I have very limited inventory of all my products as the sell through rate is slow enough where having around twenty of each item provides enough inventory to sell, and then I have enough time to order more product.

Selling printed material is a labor intensive process in the beginning. You will need to put in a fair amount of effort making contacts to sell your product, but after these initial exchanges you will find that it is a relatively self sustaining business. Through your online store you will be able to fulfill orders, and this does not take much time once you are up and running. You will also discover that local businesses are great for reordering product, and this will altogether take up even less of your time than fulfilling online orders.

T-Shirts

I have personally found the most success in my self printing business with t-shirts. There are many different groups and organizations that need t-shirts, and it can be quite easy to strike deals in person. This is a great avenue especially if you are familiar with the people and businesses in your town or city. You will be relying on their patronage, but getting the point across that you are offering a valuable service is relatively easy. You will be focusing on several different groups within your city: bands, local businesses, and group associations (Boy Scouts, community centers, etc).

Your first outreach should go to any local bands in your town. The service that you are providing to these bands is the creation of a logo or design, or licensing of one, and the printing of the material. You might have to pay the up front cost of producing the t-shirts, but this is ultimately a minor detail that can be worked out with each individual musical group. If you are struggling to think of any bands in your area, I suggest that you go out to several of your local bars and ask around. When I was getting started with this venture, I wasn't particularly aware of that many musicians, but even in my relatively small town I was able to find around six bands with relative ease. After you have identified the main groups in your town, you should make contact with each band. This is the first step in a three step process. The second step is to make a sales pitch about generating a logo or design for their group. Remember that it is relatively easy to print t-shirts, and there is no reason why a band cannot do this themselves. What you are really offering is the design and logo, and then the actual printing of the t-shirts is just icing on the cake.

When you initially meet with a band you are not going to have logos or designs ready to go. In my case, I had to meet with at least one member of each band and find what their particular 'style' was. Some of the groups were classic rock, others were metal or punk. The point is that each group had their own style, and I had to determine the type of t-shirt and design that they would want before producing any printed goods. Once I had met with a group, I would take around a week to find designs that were appealing. Since I was not creating these designs myself, I would use this week to look through Deviant Art and contact artists and discuss possibly licensing an image. Some artists have their own options to buy t-shirts and posters directly through the Deviant Art service, but I cannot recommend this because it will eat into your margins fairly significantly. After I had some samples, I would go back to each band and present the images. Most of the time, a band would find a design that they really liked. I was not dishonest with these bands, and told them that I was licensing these images, and that if they decided to go through me I would take care of all of the paperwork and licensing fees. From here we would discuss how many t-shirts they wanted and in what sizes. For example the punk rock band that I worked with skewed towards a younger audience so they needed smaller t-shirts. I would also negotiate the price at this point, which ranged from $8-$10 per t-shirt. The bands were selling t-shirts for anywhere from $15-$25 at their shows, so again this is profitable for everyone. This is step two after you've made contact, agreeing on a logo and setting the price, size, and number of items that you are going to deliver.

The last step is finding a producer for your t-shirts, and making sure that the numbers are going to work to your favor. Assuming that the band is paying $8 for each t-shirt, you will want to sell around one hundred shirts. AlliedShirts.com for example costs around $4 per shirt for one hundred shirts. The cost of licensing a design is variable, but I found myself paying between $1 and $1.50 per shirt. Depending on the deal you strike with a band, you might need to pay the up front cost to produce the t-shirts. This isn't that big of a deal if you are going to sell them to a band right away, but it is a consideration that you should be aware of. You should be prepared to pay out the initial cost to make the delivery. I was able to make around $2000 in three to four months by dealing with local bands.

What's important is that you are also going to be selling these t-shirts for long into the future. Part of the deal that I struck with nearly all the bands I dealt with was that I was going to be able to sell the t-shirts online through my Amazon store. Additionally if the band wanted any more t-shirts, they would have to go through me. This is a great way of generating passive income because the up front cost is low, the time investment is merely a matter of making contacts, and the revenue stream will persist for long into the future; it simply requires you to make that initial contact with music groups in your town or city. Additionally, keep in mind that the larger your town or city, the greater the possible revenue stream. One last thing to note about t-shirts: do not worry about bands going around you to make the t-shirts themselves. They essentially cannot do this if you either licensed the image or created it yourself. If you created it yourself then you are owed royalties on that image, and if you licensed the image then they will have to get in contact with the original artist to produce it themselves. Also, keep in mind that they are profiting greatly off of every t-shirt, even if you are selling individual shirts for $10 pop to a band. There is both the technical difficulty and a lack of reason for them to circumvent going around you to make t-shirts, so your investment is fairly safe.

The same format of finding and working out a deal to produce t-shirts can be done with local businesses. There is a key difference here though, in that typically business owners will be more aware of the costs of producing t-shirts. Also, typically they will be selling t-shirts for a far lower price than bands. While a band might sell a shirt for as much as $25 at a performance, the businesses in my area rarely sold shirts for more than $12. The problem then becomes two fold: one, convince local businesses to buy into the idea of t-shirts for their business, and two, convince them that you are a necessary part of the process to make the item. I wanted to start this section with selling directly to bands for a reason; they are far easier to negotiate with, and your value is clearer. There are a couple of ways that you can negotiate with business to further your chances of a sale, and just like with bands, you only need to strike a deal once for it to be profitable for long into the future.

For starters, you want to focus on businesses that would actually benefit from t-shirts. I have found that some of the best options are bars, and local niche businesses, like tutoring centers and gardening stores. These are businesses that are not large enough to have their own uniforms, but at the same time would benefit from the merchandise. For gardening stores and tutoring centers, you are looking at relatively small orders of around one hundred t-shirts or fewer. I believe these to be easier places to pitch to, but altogether the total revenue stream is less than a bar. The bars that I have sold t-shirts to have been repeat business because customers actively want the merchandise – I suppose it is more fashionable to wear a shirt from a bar than one from a tutoring center. For tutoring centers and gardening stores, the shirts are likely to only be used for employees. You can work around this by adjusting your pricing structure. For businesses that are not going to be selling shirts in store, I would never sell shirts for less than $15 a piece, and you should have an order of twenty shirts or more. You should note that you are not going to make a lot of profit, but what you are doing here is marketing. When other local businesses catch eye of uniforms, they might ask where they received it, and then your customers would refer back to you. The first strategy then is to try and sell shirts out of a necessity for a uniform, and the main argument is for brand awareness. In addition, the relatively small number that are you selling will incentivize businesses further, as the total cost to buy t-shirts from you will be rather minimal.

The second aspect of selling to local businesses is to focus on logos and designs that are minimalistic. These need to be custom made, so you can't rely on licensing from online artists. I found that the best way to make great logos is by using Fiveer.com. This website will do a number of tasks for a small amount of money. Essentially you offer a bounty on a small task and someone will complete the task after finding your advertisement. What's neat about this system is that it forces competition among graphic designers to create logos, and you will only have to pay for accepted work. I found this to be a great way to create a few logos to bring back to stores. This is your competitive advantage in this market; this is what you are offering that the store cannot do themselves. You are taking the time to research logos and put together a proposal of a few options for the business owner.

Selling to bars is largely the same process as selling to niche local businesses, expect you must emphasize the importance of merchandising. Making this sales pitch requires some skill, but if you can get the point across that their brand will expand if they sell merchandise, you might be able to make a sale. Personally, I used the fact that I sold to other businesses as a reason for why bars should buy shirts from me. Typically they will be buying more shirts than other local businesses, and since they are selling directly to customers you can expect far more reorders from these types of establishments. Furthermore this initial contact, even if the business does not accept your offer, will be handy in additional passive income streams found in books three and four. Keep this in mind, so even if they do not buy your t-shirts, your efforts will not be for nothing. You are making a contact that you will use again at a later time.

The last type of group that you should try and sell shirts to are local community groups. The first group I sold to was the local Boy Scout troop in my town. While the Boy Scouts of America have merchandise that they sell to troops across the country, what you are offering is more specialized. This type of process follows the same path as selling t-shirts to any other business. You can expect repeat business from these types of organizations as new members will mean re-orders of your product. Additionally, groups that focus on participation from children are going to order many different sizes of shirts because of the nature of their group – children of all sizes simply means more sales.

The take away from t-shirt sales should be that you are creating a service by taking many disparate steps of t-shirt creation and performing them for local businesses and groups. Your job is to paint a picture of your service as doing the legwork in getting the t-shirts made. Remember that even when certain groups do not order that many t-shirts, you are still making progress by making your service known. This is a great passive income stream, and if I can make this work in my relatively small town, I'm sure that no matter the population size of where you're from, you can make this work too.

Posters

The path to creating an income stream from posters through local businesses is largely the same as with t-shirts. The main difference is going to come from the type of groups that you want to appeal to. My main driver of income came from bands in my town. Since the total market for sales is far less, you want to create multiple products to sell to a single group. Focus on selling a few posters to each band in your town – and much like t-shirts you will find repeat business when their supply has been exhausted.

I should mention that you will likely find greater success from your online marketplace with posters than you will with t-shirts. Services like VistaPrint.com make it easy to place orders of all different sizes, and my particular path to getting material came from licensing interesting images found on Deviant Art. Essentially what you are doing is creating a one stop shop for numerous artists featured on Deviant Art, and selling them in a different marketplace. I have found that negotiations are slightly tougher as artists are more likely to decline licensing their images for posters. I feel this is because Deviant Art offers this exact same service, and the artist receives a far larger cut than what you will be offering. To make your sales pitch more appealing, focus on the fact that you are selling to a different group of customers. The overlap between Amazon customers and Deviant Art customers is relatively small, and by selling on Amazon they are expanding their potential reach. Also, mention that they will be credited for the work and that they can add their signature to any work that you license. I have found that a common argument from artists is to ask why they can't do this project themselves. This is where your previous venture in t-shirts pays off – you can point to your online marketplace and say that you already have a presence. You are already a retailer of these types of goods, and you have the size and influence that they do not. This is not entirely far off from the truth, even though it might be quite an embellishment. I have found this argument to be effective when trying to license an image that I really enjoy.

There is one additional avenue to selling your posters online that is not available to you when selling t-shirts. I was able to make a deal with my local Dunkin Donuts to carry prints for free in their store. These prints all have a small note indicating where customers can buy a copy for their own use. This avenue might not be available to everyone, and honestly I was quite surprised when my local Dunkin Donuts was this accommodating. If a national chain was willing to let me hang prints for with advertisements for free, I suggest that you look at your local coffee shops, or places that could benefit from free art on in store. This has proven to drive a few sales of my posters, and is worth doing because the effort needed is relatively small. You will need to spend the initial money to get the prints necessary to hang in stores, but it's a small cost for what is essentially long term free advertising.

Paperback Books

With printing paperback books on demand, you can really start to see how one passive income opportunity leads to another. The books that you should be printing are your own, and the whole process to set it up is incredibly easy. For the eBooks that you created for the Kindle store, you can enroll in a program where Amazon will print books on demand. Make sure that you set the price to be above $10 for printed material, as I have found anything lower to not be worth the effort – the margins simply aren't high enough. The eBook might still sell for just $3, but the physical book will cost more. There are a couple of other ways that you can sell printed books, but these are more risky endeavors, and they feature an upfront cost.

The general rule is that the more prints of a book at a single time, the cheaper the cost. You can use this to your advantage if you believe that you will be able to sell these books to some local businesses or community courses. This avenue is not going to be for everyone, and it requires that you have created a particular type of material. There are two main outlets for selling this material in your local town. You can either sell books to community courses where you have relevant material, or you can try and sell the books to bookstores. The path to profitability here is dependent on you ordering at least one hundred copies of a particular eBook, so you will want to negotiate with local businesses before taking the plunge.

In the case of selling material for coursework, you will want to focus on adult education programs. For example, many of adult education courses are teaching very simple skills to adults that simply have not kept up with technology. You may produce a book that teaches users how to interact and make the most out of Facebook or Evernote – these are the same types of courses that are offered for adult education. Additionally, these courses are never free, and the associated fee can be used to cover your books. This is a difficult venture and will require you to negotiate with your adult education provider in your local town. The advantage here is that these course are offered several times a year, so you can expect repeat sales if you are able to make that initial sale. I myself was not able to make this particular venture work, but that does not mean that you shouldn't give it a try. Remember, I'm from a relatively small town and really only had one outlet to sell to. If you live in a more densely populated area you will at least have more opportunities to make this type of sale.

You can also try and sell your printed books to locally owned bookstores. There are two ways to go about doing this. You can first try and broker a deal where they buy the books directly from you, and so you receive up front payment. The second method is to provide the books for free and then collect payment from the store once those books have sold through to consumers. This is a risky proposition, and it is far more likely that a book store would prefer the later scenario, where you front the cost. There is also the issue of finding a local book store, as many of these stores have closed down over the years. Still, if you have this type of local business in your area, you should try and negotiate a deal to sell your books. Be careful if you have to pay the up front cost, but this could be a venture where you find repeat sales at a high frequency.

Considerations

There are a few problem spots with printed material that you need to take into account. The main issue is that this is something that any local business can do themselves, at least in regards to t-shirts and posters. You will need to be convincing in your case that you are a necessary part of the process. I have found that emphasizing my part in licensing images to be a main driver of getting bands to agree to a deal – it makes what is essentially an easy process seem more complicated. You are providing value, but perhaps you are inflating the service that you offer. You should also consider that getting started with printing requires a lot of legwork. I have found that the best way to make any sales from shirts, posters or books is to focus on local businesses first. This will take time as you build connections and try and sell your material around. This is also one venture where there is real possibility that you have to pay an up front cost for merchandise. Even in the case of bands that buy shirts from you, you may need to front the cost before receiving payment. Just be prepared to make that initial payment if necessary, and also be weary of buying printed material to sell for later when you don't have a buyer set up. This is a good way to be left with lots of inventory that you will have difficult moving later on. You might be able to sell it through all of it on your Amazon store eventually, but it will take time and you will have to hold onto the inventory before it sells.

You should also take into consideration the process of paying taxes on this income. The ventures in book one were rather straight forward with how you pay taxes since organizations would collect your tax identification number and send you the proper documentation. This is still going be the case with items that you sell through Amazon, but for selling items locally you will need to do these taxes yourself. If you are able to drive physical sales through in-person negotiations, I highly suggest that you find a tax accountant that can help you with your filing. There are many nuances to filing taxes when you are selling directly to consumers. For example, you are technically supposed to file every quarter, or four times a year. I cannot offer you specific tax advice so it is best to contact a local professional.

Chapter 6: Instagram

A Matter of Partnerships

Instagram might not seem like a great place to generate an income stream, and in fact it is not. The way to make money through Instagram is through partnerships with companies that pay for product placement in your photos. This venture is very similar to YouTube in that you need to build an audience before you can start making money. You should note that even more so than YouTube, this is a fairly active investment. You will need to update your account regularly, and also early on you will be the one reaching out to companies.

The types of Instagram accounts that generate revenue through product promotion are very particular; they focus on selfies. Instagram accounts that have amazing shots of nature and are regularly updated rarely earn the type of revenue that selfie accounts do. This means that you need to be both outgoing and rather photogenic to make this avenue work. That being said, the active part of updating your account is rather modest. You must simply take several shots a week and keep your account updated. Building a community through Instagram has the added benefit of serving nearly all other income streams detailed in books one and two. You can increase your YouTube following, drive book sales, increase print sales and more through gaining momentum on Instagram.

The promotion that you do for companies through Instagram will be difficult at first. You will need to reach out these companies, point to your followers, and make a case for product promotion. In the beginning it is likely that this does not manifest in the form of hard currency. You are more likely to simply receive products for free as long as they are featured on your account. This might be displeasing to some, but it is a form of compensation – you just have to be comfortable with how you are receiving payment. As your following grows and you gain more views for each upload, there will be real money on the table. Your success early on is going to depend on your existing presence online. If you already have a following on YouTube, it is likely that you can start making money on Instagram rather quickly. If you do not, it could take up to a year to get the necessary amount of followers to get any brand promotion at all, whether that be cash payments or free products.

Building an Audience

There are many ways to build your audience on Instagram, but to be frank some of us will have a greater chance of success out of the gate than others. I am of course referring to how naturally attractive the owner of the Instagram account is. You should not feel as though you need to look like a model, but attractiveness helps build followers; it's just a fact. That being said, the selfies that you do take do not need to focus entirely on yourself. There is another avenue you can take, and that is to merely photograph interesting subjects whenever you take a selfie. Also note that the total number of followers that you need to be able to sell products is not at all large. You will only need around 500 followers before you can start contacting companies and start asking for product promotion on your profile.

The two main drivers of Instagram followers are either the beauty/style of the person holding the account, or the beautiful and unique scenes that they are regularly able to capture. If you happen to be extremely genetically gifted, you might want to try just taking several selfies a day and uploading them to see how many followers you can attract. This is a very low effort way to build followers, and for the vast majority of us we will not find success with such ease. We need to be more creative to gain followers, and take interesting photos that are not necessarily about the person in the selfie. For example, there are many successful accounts that focus on niche topics like applying makeup or demonstrating exercise routines. These are Instagram accounts that are almost like a tutorial, or a teaching experience. Essentially you are trying to form a hook for your audience, something unique that you can offer that others can't. In the case of makeup, focus on unusual styles or designs of a particular angle, like making yourself look like a known celebrity. For exercise accounts or tutorial accounts, focus on teaching skills that will better your followers. You simply need something that other Instagram accounts do not offer.

If you cannot make yourself or one of your skills the product, you will need to make up the slack by making sure that your background subjects are as interesting as possible. For example, some successful accounts feature a number of selfies along with shots of nature. These are accounts that have their popularity because of the specific shots the Instagram account holder can take. If you live in a rural area, focus on shots of beauty or artistic expression. If you are an expert chef, focus on taking shots of your finished creations. This angle focuses on creating a pleasing image for your audience, instead of necessarily you as the subject of your photos. You will still want to include selfies so that you are recognizable with the account – this is a necessity as it makes it easier to sell to advertisers.

Reaching out to Brands

If you have 500 or more followers, you can start to get in contact with companies that might be interested in promoting their products on your account. It is important that you reach out to lesser known brands, as these are the companies that are in need of any type of promotion. A well known chain will not have much interest in working with a small account, but a relatively new brand or store will be more than happy to at least negotiate some type of product promotion. When you reach out to companies, focus on companies that represent what your channel focuses on. If your main attractor is your beautiful selfies, focus on glamor products. If your main product is nature, focus on brands that are synonymous with natural products. The key here is to identify your own personal brand and try and sell that image to companies that will want to work with you.

You should note that some companies are more likely to work with Instagram accounts than others. You may want to take a day and look at accounts that work with brands and see what companies are already interested in being featured on Instagram. Additionally, if you do not have 500 followers, or even if you do but want to make clear that you have an audience, indicate to companies that your online presence is more than just your Instagram account. You should include your YouTube account, your Amazon store and your eBooks as a sign that you have a greater online presence than merely this one outlet. If you find any distaste in the idea of the phrase 'personal brand', I can share this sentiment, but this is essentially what drives online marketing. You need to be more than just a single account; you need to have synergy between all aspects of your online presence. Each plays into the other, and this will be important as you are lifting your Instagram account off the ground.

Considerations

Not all ventures are designed for everyone, and this is certainly true when it comes to Instagram. You need to actively participate in your account, replying to comments and interacting with your community. This requires a very special type of personality; you need to be outgoing and also understanding of your audience. You need to play to what people want from your account, which is a sense of belonging and place. You need to keep your account updated very frequently, as stagnation on an account is a huge reason for a decline in participation. You are also exposing yourself as a minor celebrity, and perhaps even more so than YouTube, you are exposing yourself to all of the terrible elements of the Internet. I'm referring to the people that will insult you, make fun of your image, your skills or whatever you are trying to accomplish on your account. You will need to have thick skin to make this work, so if you're a naturally shy or timid person, be mindful of what an active Instagram account entails.

Chapter 7: Creating Online Courses

Not as Complicated as You Think

When I first considered the prospect of creating an online course, I thought the whole process to be daunting. It entails creating valuable material that can be used to teach others a specific skill. I wasn't sure where to start, what type of materials would be useful, or even sure what exactly I should teach. I'm happy to say that the whole process is much easier than you might initially assume. This largely comes down to a single website, Udemy.com, where I highly urge you host any online courses. This website is the number one provider of online courses and features everything from auto repair to computer programming. You can create a course on literally any subject, and they provide many tools to help you in creating your course. Before you embark on this endeavor, I highly urge you to take a look at the website and see the format for some of the popular courses. There are a few components, including video tutorials and coursework that can be completed either alongside the videos, or as homework assignments.

Individual courses range in price and length. You can expect to price your course between $50 and $200, but also note that you can offer sales as frequently as you want. The list price does not necessarily need to be the permanent price of your course either, so if you find it is not selling you can either set a permanent price cut or run sales very frequently. I have found that many courses will overprice their courses and run sales continually – I suggest you don't go this route as it seems to underscore the value of the course being provided. The length of each course ranges between three and twenty-five hours, depending on the subject. There is certainly a strong correlation between the type of material and how long the course is, however I have seen very complicated subjects covered in as little as three hours, so there isn't a clear cut rule for how long you should make your courses.

You might be wondering about creating material and the video required to make a course. I have found that one of the best ways for beginners to start is to create a course entirely in PowerPoint. You can even use the Open Broadcast Software (OBS) discussed in book one for recording your desktop and your voice. These videos are easier to produce, however they are associated with lower cost courses. If you intend on charging more, you should be prepared to film yourself and not just your desktop. Also, there is an expectoration that coursework is produced at a fairly high quality. You will need to make strong edits so that your material flows nicely. If you have already tried to make a successful YouTube channel, then you will have experience with video editing. Again, these passive income streams all play into each other, both in terms of promotion and the shared skills that they feature. Learning video editing for one venture will carry over to another one, as is the case here.

Your Audience Starts from Your Other Endeavors

You cannot expect to upload a course and then have students buy it right away. There are *so many* courses on Udemy that you will need something to attract customers. This is where your other endeavors will play a huge part in your success, particularly your eBook writing. I highly urge that any relent eBooks have links in them to your online courses. If you already have published eBooks that do not refer to your coursework, you can go to Amazon and add the relevant links. Your Instagram and YouTube accounts should also feature your Udemy courses, provided they are all somewhat related.

Truly the only way to make sure that you gain customers is by providing a useful course, but more importantly you need to have each venture refer to your other projects. This is particularly the case with Udemy, where essentially no courses are ever found through the search function. For example, suppose that you are offering an extremely niche course, such as a history lesson on the first three months of the French Revolution. Even though you are looking at a specific time period, there are going to be dozens of courses just like yours. They might not focus on the first three months, but the general topic will be similar enough that you will face lots of competition. There is absolutely no reason for a customer to click on your course instead of someone else's. Simply put, you need referrals to your lessons; otherwise you will not be able to attract customers.

Teaching What You Know

Since your views are coming from your other projects, this immediately limits what your coursework should be about. You will need to focus on the projects that you have already completed through YouTube, eBooks, Instagram, etc. Students are going into your courses knowing you for a particular skill that you have already shown through these other mediums, and they will expect that your coursework features this same material. It is one thing to feature a skill, but to teach that skill is entirely different. An Udemy course is a *huge* investment of your time. The total cost to entry monetarily might be very low, but you cannot underestimate exactly how long it will take you to finish a course. I would expect that a five to ten hour course takes up to a full month to finish, however keep in mind that online courses have some of the longest tails for passive income. You will find that as long as you continue to promote your courses, that they will generate revenue for a very long time.

If your YouTube channel focuses on your personality, and your Instagram account is entirely based around your beautiful genetic predisposition, you might have some difficultly in figuring out exactly what you should be offering to your students. Trust me when I say that you have more skills than you know. From how to write and publish an eBook, to the history of your local state, you can teach just about anything. Remember that the real driver of your courses is not just the material covered, but your own personality and your outreach in other markets. Provided you have made that outreach, you will find that you can attract customers to any type of material that you wish to provide.

One of the more ingenious ways to make a number of course is to focus on projects and not necessarily broader topics overall. This is good advice for a first time teacher, as breaking down a larger topic can be difficult. For example, if you are teaching algebra as a whole, it can be difficult to know exactly where to start your course and where to end. Do you include trigonometry, graphing algebraic equations; should these be courses of their own? When you focus on individual projects, like rebuilding the engine to a car, or renovating a home, you have clearer start and stop points. It becomes easier to organize your thoughts and structure your lessons. Even if you do decide to teach a much boarder topic, focus on trying to break it down by the ultimate objective that you are trying to teach. Instead of trying to teach the history of the American Revolution, answer a question like, why did the French get involved in this conflict? In trying to answer this complex question, you can come up with a lesson plan that is more clear than if you tried to tackle the subject as a whole.

If you find yourself wanting to create many different lessons on a variety of subjects, or you are just not sure where to start because you are bustling with ideas, consider referring to your other outlets and see what your audience wants. Look deeply at your Instagram account and see what topics garner the most comments, or look at your eBook sales to see what is most appealing to your base. Remember, you are selling all of these products to the same customer base, so focus on what your customers already want from you. You can also try and experiment with your other accounts and throw material out there and see what sticks. Make a video about a topic that you are considering creating a course on and then see how your audience reacts. This is potentially a great way to gauge enthusiasm for the topics you want to cover.

The Art of Instruction

In college, I offered both tutoring services for academia and for music. I was relatively inexperienced but I had the mindset that it would be very easy to teach. After all I knew the material extremely well; how difficult could it be to teach what I already knew? What I found is what many first time teachers come to realize, teaching is something that everyone thinks they are good at but nearly everyone is terrible at in the beginning. Teaching is an acquired skill, and I would almost recommend looking for an Udemy course on how to make efficient Udemy courses. You will absolutely need to prepare yourself for how to teach courses, and the best way to do this is to practice with a loved one or friend. Go over the material that you plan on teaching and see if your loved one or friend can understand the overall lesson you have crafted. Ask for criticism and see what you can improve about your lesson overall. This should be the step that you take before you start recording yourself for online lessons, as this is an essential part of creating the best possible coursework. You are sure to find that material you thought you explained well went completely over the head of the person you were instructing – this is very normal. I am a proponent that teaching only improves if you allow yourself to hone in on this particular skill. You should take the feedback provided very seriously, and do not treat it as an indictment on your ability to teach – truly no one is great at this from the very beginning.

There are a number of common mistakes that teachers make that you can avoid. For starters, you will want to outline exactly where your course is heading. You have a final objective, but you need to list all of the material that you will cover up until that point. What you are doing is building a roadmap for your students, and showing them how each topic plays into the next. For example, if you are teaching a course on programming, you would indicate that you need to understand the first topic of naming a variable before you can move onto other lessons. Point out to students exactly what material they need to master before they can move on to the next step in a course. First time teachers also tend to move through material too quickly, so focus on moving very slowly. You are trying to impart knowledge to a wide mass of people, but you should be aiming for the least common denominator of student. Know that students that are able to comprehend material more quickly will be able to speed up a video to one and half times (recommend on many instructional videos), so your objective should always be to speak to the student that is most likely to have the most trouble with understanding your lesson. This is why it is so important to practice live in front of someone so that you can get immediate feedback. You should never upload a course until it has been looked at by someone that is not yourself. You have many innate blind spots when listing your material and you will not fully comprehend what is so difficult about the subject that you are trying to teach. Lastly, first time teachers often have difficulty with either making their courses too fun or too dry – this is perhaps the most difficult part to master. You need to keep your course interesting throughout, but load it with too many jokes and you will find that students will zone out just as much as if the material was too dry and boring. This might sound counterintuitive but think back to the teachers that you have had throughout your life. The best teachers had a perfect mix of seriousness and humor, and you've seen plenty of teachers that bend the scale either too much in one direction or the other. For this too you will need an outside viewer to really grasp how your lessons should flow, and whether or not they are loaded with too many jokes, or if they feel too somber throughout.

Considerations

Many of the ventures in books one and two of the Passive Income series require an outgoing personality, and creating online coursework is no exception. You will need to be enthusiastic and strike the right tone with your audience. You will need to find the middle ground between too many jokes without enough instruction, and too boring of a voice while focusing only on the lesson. Creating a course is *a lot* of work, even more so than creating a number of YouTube videos or writing several eBooks. It is a commitment of time, but also that time is very difficult work – it is mentally exhausting. Consider all of the work that goes into making a course, and also the huge obstacle of all of the video editing that needs to be done. As you are creating your first courses, consider aiming for shorter projects. This will allow you to get your feet wet and understand the process of creating coursework. It will also allow you to get feedback from your audience and adjust for future courses. If you make your first course a twenty-plus hour endeavor, then editing that project when you get comments is going to be far more time intensive.

Please take to heart my comments about how online courses find their students. There are virtually no courses that blow up by themselves, no matter how unique the subject. Creating online courses is not a starting point, but rather part of a larger path towards creating your online brand. If you have not created any eBooks, made a YouTube channel, or garnered any Instagram subscribers, focus on these ventures first. You will be hard pressed to sell your course unless you are starting with an established audience. Online courses are a great way to generate a long term revenue stream, but it must be built upon the foundation of an audience that you gained through other means.

Conclusion

Thank you again for downloading *Passive Income: Part Two.*

I hope that you have enjoyed the first two parts of the Passive Income series. The goal of parts one and two is to build passive income streams through creating your own online brand. From YouTube videos to online courses, these are ventures that build on top of your previous efforts. Not all ventures will be suitable for everyone, and the first two books in this series do benefit the more outgoing among us, however you have opportunities to create income streams through a print per demand and eBooks if you feel too shy for these other ventures.

Please note that all of the passive income ideas listed in books one and two require very little money to start, but they all require time and effort. This is the trade off of in the first half of this series, and it truly benefits those of us that have more time than money. If you have enjoyed the first half of this series, I ask that you continue with books three and four. These additional resources will focus on more traditional passive income streams, and will require a monetary investment but far less of your time than the first half of this series. The best way to generate a sustainable passive income stream is to focus on the projects that appeal to your sensibilities and skills – there are enough proposals here that you should find several ventures that will work for you.

I have outlined numerous projects to generate passive income, but remember that to truly master any one project I suggest that you find a mentor. Please refer to the end of every chapter to find a recommended mentor, and I urge that you do not veer too far from this list. For every great mentor, there are another dozen that will provide less than adequate instruction. Please find links below to the additional books in this series. I offer the same high quality instruction, but with additional avenues for generating passive income, along with all of the considerations and costs to entry.

Lastly if you enjoyed this book, it would be much appreciated if you could leave a review on Amazon. The best way for this book to make its way into the hands of more readers is through truthful reviews about this work. Please write what you liked about this book and what could be improved upon. Any and all feedback is helpful as I continue to serve the needs of my readership.

Thank you and good luck!

Passive Income

Incredible Ideas of How to Make Money While You Sleep

Part Three

Passive Income Series

Part One:

    EBook Writing

    YouTube Ad Revenue

    Stock Photos

    Audio Samples

Part Two:

    Print per Demand

    Instagram

    Creating Online Courses

Part Three:

    P2P Lending

    Creating Apps

    Joint Venture Partnerships

Part Four:

    Informational Products

    Affiliate Marketing

    Dividend Stocks

Introduction

I want to thank you and congratulate you for downloading Passive Income: Part Three.

Welcome to part three of the four-part Passive Income series. The focus of parts one and two are to generate passive income through minimal monetary investment. There is a high trade off, and although the monetary cost to investment is low, parts one and two focused on hard labor for long-term income streams. Parts three and four of this series will focus on larger scale investments that will require both labor and monetary investment. These are avenues of generating passive income that is more certain to turn into revenue streams, but the cost to investment makes these choices unsuitable for some. If you are just getting started with generating passive income and feel that some of the choices in this book are prohibitively expensive, I highly urge you to read through parts one and two of this series; links to parts one and two can be found after the conclusion.

The focus of part three is to generate long term passive income through a combination of hard work and some monetary investment. There are multiple price points to get started, and depending on the skills that you may already possess, some options may prove to be less expensive than original thought. This book will discuss how to generate revenue through P2p lending, creating an app/s, and through joint venture partnerships. These are investments that I have participated in myself, and while some money down is required, there are pricing options available, so you get started even if you don't have that much to investment. As we move into these later investments, you will notice that they mimic more traditional investments but are accomplished on a smaller scale. These are invented that any American household can participate in, and with the trade off for more monetary investment and less labor, these inventions will overall take less of your time than what was provided in parts one and two of this series.

Passive income is a process that builds on your past efforts, and the following investments will prove to be no different. In each case, you will only be earning small returns at first, but with reinvestment, this will build into a larger revenue stream over time. Mimicking traditional forms of investments, there will be an inherent mental roadblock to getting started – the initial returns will seem too small to be worth your effort. This is a completely normal aspect of human behavior and is, in fact, the reason that so many Americans do not invest, to begin with. There is no such thing as easy money, but these are investments that are trading labor for money and time. By merely sitting back, watching your investment grow, and then reinvesting that money, you will come to find your passive revenue stream can supplement your main income quite significantly. It is just a matter of getting over the hump of starting with investment and parting with your hard-earned money for enough time to watch an investment grow.

Humans have innate difficulty grasping the concept of compound interest. We must truly see a written plan for generating returns before we can understand the benefit of the investment. We simply have not evolved in such a way to grasp this concept intuitively. Take for example the case of the penny problem; a classic example of the difficulty of understanding interest over time. Suppose for a moment that a man offered you a choice, you could either have one million dollars today or the sum of a penny being doubled every day for thirty days. If you're familiar with this problem, then you will know that the second choice is far wiser than the first. If you have never been presented this question, then it will jump out at you to take the first choice. You will have to logically think through the consequences to consider the second choice to be a better option; we simply cannot see the benefit of a penny doubling unless we do the math. This example drives home a couple of key points to investing, with the first being that compound interest is something our brains handle poorly and needs to be written out to be fully understood. The second point is just as important to investing. However, we must sacrifice time to gain interest, as time is an integral component of investment.

The penny problem illustrates the benefits of compound interest, with a penny doubling each day for thirty days generating some ten times greater than the first choice of the immediate money in hand. Once the math has been written out the second choice is a no-brainer, but there is a hidden cost that is often missed in this example, the time to gain returns. The first option of the penny problem offers a million dollars on day one, and while the second may offer far more money, it will take a full month to earn that additional money. This is the hurdle that you must get over to generate passive income for long into the future. Think about all of the times that you forwent later payment for the upfront sum. From buying smaller packages of goods at the supermarket, to simply not starting to invest until recently. Parts one and two of this series had very hands-on methods of generating passive income, so even when the money was not immediate, there was in effect the feeling of moving forward with a project. As you continue to read and learn about additional ventures for passive income, the largest hurdle, in the beginning, will be the feeling that your money is at risk when it is not in your hands. Furthermore, the time you are separate from your investment money can feel as though you are making a mistake. Consider that in the penny problem if you had taken the second choice how you would feel each and every day until you received payment. You would be battling the thought that you should have taken the first option. Even though you know the second choice is clearly more beneficial, the feeling that it is riskier, that you will not receive any money at all, and the thought of what you could have done with the initial million dollars will be battling for dominance in your mind. This is the thought process you must overcome – you must think of your investments with a long-term outlook and internalize that forgoing upfront cash for larger returns later is the only way to build your passive income stream.

As you continue reading, I want you to keep the penny problem in mind. Each method for generating passive income is demonstrative of the penny problem but on a very small scale. You must be comfortable with parting your money, taking a little risk on initial investment, and always reinvesting the principal investment with interest. If you can think this way, you will have matched the thought process of a seasoned investor. Continue reading, keeping in mind our initial bias towards upfront payment, and I'm sure that you will be able to generate passive income through these ventures for long into the future.

Chapter 8: P2P Lending

What is P2P Lending?

With ever increasingly diminished purchasing power and the average American household saddled with at least some debt, there has been a recent boom in the economy. That boom comes from the short-term loan industry. There is no doubt that you have seen payday loan stores in your local town or city. There are more payday loan storefronts in the United States than there are McDonald's. This is an incredible feat, if also a scary one. Payday loans offer very short term loans for exorbitant interest rates. There has recently been pushback on the incredibly high interest rates, but it seems likely that the industry will win out in most states, keeping their business practices largely unchanged.

Regardless of your feelings about payday loans, there is one inarguable truth – it is a desired and necessary service for many Americans. Even with regulation and strict codes of conduct, this would not diminish the serious appetite for borrowing in the United States. Payday loans are a fairly safe investment for the lender, as they typically either require collateral or documentation showing the borrower is gainfully employed. With no other option, payday loans are the dominant short-term lender in the country, but there is competing business that is gaining moment, peer to peer lending.

Peer to peer lending uses the resource of the internet to connect lenders to borrowers across the country and the globe. Your part in gaining a steady stream of passive income comes from lending to borrowers. You are essentially filling the role of a payday loan store, except your interest rates will be far lower. I wanted to start with a strong emphasis on payday loans because it demonstrates the demand for lending, as there are always borrowers in need. Online lending sites are a place of refuge for families seeking short-term loans but are wary of the high-interest rates on payday loans. The average annual interest rate (APR) for online lending sites is about 5.9%, far lower than the double-digit costs of borrowing in person at a payday store. There is little reason for families not to first look online for loans, except for one problem, there simply are not enough lenders to go around.

Your part in online lending is finding borrowers with reputable credit and lending sums of money ranging from one hundred up to five or ten thousand dollars. The interest rates on these loans are fairly modest, but if you continually reinvest your principal investment plus interest, you can expect to build a healthy income stream. This is a passive income stream that requires minimal maintenance, and after you've conducted a few dozen loans, it becomes quite easy what to look for in a borrower. For example, many online lenders will have a form for indicating what the loans are to be used for. There are some clear red flags depending on what is checked in that box, and as you become more comfortable with the system, you can take greater risks in lending but will be rewarded with higher interest rates.

Peer to peer lending is a viable investment because the demand is there, and the barrier to entry is fairly minimal. There are some online lending sites that you can participate in, ranging from the altruistic to digital storefronts that mimic payday loan stores. Some sites will have predetermined interest rates, while others will allow you to set the interest rate yourself. In making a loan, you work out the details with the borrower for when you can expect payment, but it should be noted that collecting on debt is extremely difficult. Often there is no binding contract stating the borrower must pay you back, and instead, you are relying on their past borrowing history on that particular website. Even if there is an enforceable contract, the cost of trying to enforce that contract is prohibitive and often outweighs the cost of the loan itself. It is for these reasons that you need to be careful about exactly whom you lend to, however, once part way have a sense for the type of borrower that you want, this passive income stream requires minimal upkeep.

How much can I expect to earn?

How much you can expect to earn is a question of how much risk you want to take on, as well as how much you are willing to lend to borrowers. You can expect that on a five hundred dollar loan, that at the end of the month you are collecting around forty dollars of interest. Again, this is variable depending on the site and the borrower, but this is a good ballpark figure. While that sum, a mere forty dollars for dealing with the thought of potentially losing five hundred dollars crossing your mind for thirty days might be too much to bear for some people, this is essentially money earned merely through the passage of time. Your upfront investment is then primarily the money you lend, and risk associated with the loan, and the time that you do not have access to that money. For example, if made a five hundred dollar loan, you are forgoing the opportunity to use that money for other opportunities until you receive payment. It is a consideration that you must take into account, but for a starting milestones investment, peer to peer lending is highly recommended. Being able to choose the amount of risk you want to expose yourself to a feature not offered by many other investment opportunities. Determining the risk on a stock, for example, is much more difficult, but by merely looking at the site's history with a borrower, you can easily make a determination for how risky the investment is.

I urge you to start with only the safest loans as you get started, meaning someone that has used a particular site some twenty times or more. These are borrowers that you can depend on, as clearly their need for the service will drive them to pay back loans. You should start with websites like Lendingclub.com and Prosper.com – these sites offer loans for anything from building a deck to your house, to making a payment on a mortgage. What's important as you start is that you veer away from alterity lending sites. These are sites that do have interest rates, but they are very low, sometimes as low as 2% APR. Lenders become involved in these sites because they want to help their fellow man and aren't 'necessarily intended in making the greatest returns possible. For your purposes, you are trying to minimize risk and still collect interest on payments – sticking to 5-10%; APR will accomplish both goals.

You can expect that over the course of a year, that if you invest around three thousand dollars, you can earn between two hundred and five hundred dollars of interest. You should process this as not necessarily having earned five hundred dollars, but rather that you now have the opportunity to invest thirty-five hundred dollars in peer to peer lending, This is the best way to drive a possible revenue from lending, always reinvesting the interest on top of the principle loan. If you can consistently do this, you will find that you are making a good deal of money by around year three of four. Additionally, you can take more and more risk and spread out your investments when you are investing a sum this great, allowing you to earn more through higher interest rates. The borrowers will always be in need, so you will never run into a situation where you log into a website and simply cannot find a borrower. Simply put, right now there are far more people asking for money than there are lending money – there will always be an opportunity, and the power of the negation currently sits in the hands of the lenders.

How much risk is involved?

Peer to peer lending can be a risky proposition if you are not careful. The legal recourse you have for getting repayment is not a good option, and the cost to litigate any unpaid loan will often be more than the loan is worth. There are some ways in which you can mitigate risk and still make a good profit, but first, you must keep in mind the two primary components that will form your risk: the APR of the loan and the borrowing history of who you are lending to. For example, the higher the APR that you set, and the longer term the loan is, the greater the chance you have of a borrower walking out on loan. At some point, the amount of interest that has earned on top of their account will indicate that it is simply easier for them to walk away than to try and repay the loan. This is one of the main drivers for why you will want to set your loans to fairly low rates, as it incentivizes the borrower to pay you back – you are fair, and it is an amount that they can pay back. You may be wondering why a borrower would enter an agreement that they couldn't possibly pay back, and this goes back to the supply and demand of borrowers and lenders. There are simply more people requesting loans than there are seeking to lend out to others. This puts so much of the power in the hands of the lender that often they can charge whatever interest rates they want, provided it is within the rules of whatever lending site they are using. You will also note that the set APR should be about how risky the borrower is, but the APR should always be fair. There are enough lending sites where a borrower will feel compelled to walk away from a loan if they are not getting a 'fair shake.'

The second primary component of determining risk is the borrowing history of a borrower. This gets into a somewhat messy issue with online lending sites, as it can be a real challenge to get an accurate picture of a borrower's credit. Some sites will require a credit report to start borrowing, while others require information filled out through a survey, with the implication being that the borrower could mislead the lender on this form. They might indicate that their income is greater than it truly is, or even show that they are employed when they are not. The internet offers the ability to lend to many people, but it also comes with all of the standard hazards of the internet, primarily being that you don't' know who you are dealing with. As you are starting, I highly suggest that you focus on borrowers that have an established reputation with a particular site. Look for borrowers that have taken out loans ten to twenty times before, and note how long it took to pay back those loans. If you have the option to set the interest rate, you should set it according to the past loans that the borrower has received – this will ensure a greater chance of success with your particular loan. Also, you can probe a borrower to determine what they need the loan for. Most sites will require a borrower to list the purpose for the loan, but this will not necessarily list enough information. If you are not satisfied with the amount of information going into a loan, don't' take the loan and merely ask the borrower for more information.

I have found that there are two primary types of loans that you lenders can participate in. The first is the type of borrower that is merely trying to preserve their way of life. I have found these types of loans to be a fairly safe investment. These types of borrowers are merely trying to pay bills and will need repeated use of a lending site to make ends meet until they get out of their rough patch. You can capitalize on this by understanding their need and using it to manage the risk of someone walking out on loan. These types of borrowers do tend to pay back their loans quite quickly, which is another consideration, mainly because it reduces the total amount of interest. It also means that you will need to participate in more loans to make returns, as once a loan is paid back you will no longer be earning interest.

The other type of borrower is trying to make money from your loan. These are an individual that are using the money from a loan to invest in a business or to start some other venture. Not all of these loans are risky, but in general, there is far more risk associated with individuals trying to make money on loan. A relatively safe investment in this vein is someone that needs a loan to get a job. This type of loan occurs quite often, and is characterized by an individual needing clothing for a job interview, or merely needs to pay for a bus pass to interview for jobs. This individual *is* trying to make money from a loan, but the venture they are participating in is relatively low risk. Getting a job is not a wildly risky way of using a loan. The second type of person tiring to make money from a loan is far riskier – these are individuals that are trying to invest on borrowed money. They might be trying to start a business, or are merely paying maintenance on their business. Even with an established borrowing history, I would be extremely wary of anyone asking for money for investment. The number of truly brilliant entrepreneurs out there is extremely limited, and the prospect that you have miracles found someone that knows what they are doing is slim to none. These types of plans do offer the chance to set the interest rates fairly high, but again this just increases the possibility that someone is not going to be able to pay you back.

To mitigate risk beyond being selective with what borrowers you select and what rates of interest you decide to choose, whether based on the site or if they are set you, you can also lend to many different parties. Suppose that you have one thousand dollars for investment. If you lend this money to a single borrower, you have tied up your total investment money in a single loan, and if that loan sours then you stand to lose the entire investment. If you had split the investment money into two or three loans, to two or three different people, then you are mitigating risk merely by spreading your risk across multiple parties. I don't' want you to get the idea that many loans are not paid back, but simply that there is inherent risk associated with lending, and you must always consider the possibility of someone walking away from a loan. You must consider that when you spread out your total investment money, might be reducing risk, but you are also increasing the total amount of upkeep and maintenance for gaining income from these loans. Each loan that you participate in requires research into the borrower. It requires determining an interest rate and reviewing when you can expect payment. Early on, this can be quite a time intensive task, as you will want to be careful with exactly whom you are lending to.

Making P2P Lending into a Sustainable Income Stream

You can start with peer to peer lending with as low as just a few hundred dollars, but this will require a lot of work on your part. You will need to make lots of little loans, and the smaller the loan, the faster that it will be paid back. You might only receive a few days of interest on a small loan, making the whole endeavor not very profitable, and meaning that you need to engage more with these online lending sites. You essentially have two factors that will determine how much upkeep and maintenance you want to keep on your account. These factors are the total number of people that you lend to, and how long or how large these loans are. The more people you loan to, and the smaller the sums, the more maintenance work you are creating for yourself. You will have to constantly be loaning out money to make any revenue, and so this passive income stream can become quite active, needing up to several hours of work each week. This method comes with far less risk, but the time required should be a consideration.

You can also lend to fewer parties and in greater amounts for longer periods of time. This will require less upkeep on your part, and the interest that you collect is larger. For example, you might plan a six-month loan, and so for those six months, you have fairly little work to do with the borrower. Additionally, each day that you are not paid back, you are earning interest.

When you commit to many short term loans, it is impossible to earn interest every day. There will simply be a deal between how frequently you can get out your loans, reducing your total profitability. There are a lot of considerations here for how much risk you want to take on, so you will have to think carefully about how comfortable you will be with lending out money and for how long you can not see that money and still feel comfortable.

As you start and get a feel for peer to peer lending, I suggest you start with short term loans at modest interest rates to get a feel for the system. Once you have a sizable investment found a few thousand dollars, I would start to take on more risk. Do this wisely by making loans of six months or greater, as these loans will require upfront research and then little maintenance beyond the initial work you put in. You must make sure that you are comfortable with parting with your money for this period of time. When I started in peer to peer lending, I was constantly worried about whether or not I would be paid back – this is a feeling that subsides after making a few loans, but it the beginning this is a heavy burden that you may have to deal with. Some people are very good at compartmentalizing their feelings and will not think about a loan that they have given out. If this describes you, you are a great candidate for making long-term loans. If not, build up your trust in the system with short term loans, until you feel comfortable with longer-term lending. You will need to aim for longer term lending in the long run, as this is truly the only way to generate a truly *passive* income stream.

Considerations

Parts one and two of the *Passive Income* series focused on up-front labor for long-term returns. We are not in the territory of less labor but an increased monetary investment. Peer to peer lending should be your first option for monetary investment as the cost to start very low. However, this brings the burden of risk in the loans that you do make. I believe that I am naturally a very nervous person, and so making the transition to long-term loans was fairly difficult for me. I constantly thought about the idea that perhaps borrowers would not pay me back. This is thought that eventually subsided after I made enough loans, but it is a consideration that you should have as you start. If you are feeling quite nervous about the install loans that you make, take solace in the idea that eventually you will feel more comfortable with the process. I also want you to note that you will have to feel comfortable with the idea of parting with your money for some period because this is a necessary skill for other types of investments in parts three and four of this series. If you can get used to lending now and parting with your money, it will make future endeavors far easier.

You should note that if you participate in peer to peer lending, your tax filing will become significantly more complicated. Even if you are lending fairly small sums of money and your interest earned is not massive, you are far more likely to be audited by the IRS. I urge you to contact an accountant and go over your filing. Depending on how long it takes for an investment to pay back the principle plus interest, you will have vastly different tax rates. Also, depending on what your household income is, this will affect the tax rate on your interest as well. Along with these added burdens do come some benefits, as investments that do not earn you profit can be counted as deductions, and are separate from the standard deductions on your tax filing. These deductions also carry over year to year as long as the investor does not pay back the principle amount. There are many other details for filing your taxes when dealing with peer to peer lending, so please contact a professional before you file.

Chapter 9: Creating Apps

The Rise of a Billion Dollar Marketplace

Sometimes I can hardly believe that the iPhone is less than a decade old. Released in 2008, the iPhone propelled the smartphone industry to new heights and created an entirely new marketplace in the process. There has been tremendous innovation in smartphones, and it has disrupted nearly every industry in some way. The smartphone must be a consideration to marketers, to newspapers and video game developers. This was facilitated by the creation of the Apple and Google marketplaces. These are digital storefronts that make billions each and every year. I'm sure that you are already aware of this, but what you might not know is what the main drivers for profit in this market.

I define the types of apps on smartphone marketplaces as either being utility-based or interactive games. Utility apps are described by podcast apps, grammar checkers, messaging clients and information services like Facebook and news sites. Utility apps do not make that much money overall, and often the point of creating an app is for a promotion of a more established business, such as Facebook. Utility apps generate revenue through one of three ways. They can be gated by a defined cost to entry, generate revenue through ads or are merely trying to attract users. The first two cases of generating revenue are quite clear. The third is a little odd, in that there is no real revenue being generating, and often there isn't' a *plan* for revenue to be generated. A company is merely trying to attract users so that the firm looks more attractive for outside investment – these companies worry about monetization at a later time. A perfect example of this is either Instagram or SnapChat, apps created by companies that were absorbed by much larger firms.

The true money makers on the app stores are interactive games. These are slightly different than passive games, similar to Foursquare or popular geotagging games – passive games mostly run in the background and do not require much input from the more play. This means that they do not generate that much ad revenue, and they typically do not have that many in-app purchases, plus customers are not as induced to spend money on the app because they simply do not engage with it for a lot of time each day. It is in interactive games that Apple and Google make a fortune. This is the avenue that you should participate in for making money through creating smartphone apps. Games can be wildly profitable, and even modestly successful ones can make tens of thousands of dollars. There are three business models for making revenue from games – they are either gated by a single purchase, generate revenue through ads, or make money through in-app purchases. The extremely heavy competition has largely made gated games unsuccessful.

To warrant a download for many users, the initial download has to be free, limiting your choices to making money through ad revenue or in-app purchases.

The games that produce the most revenue have in-app purchases that allow a player to bypass levels or gain a leg up on their competition. Interestingly, 95% of all players do not engage with in-app purchases. Only one twenty will ever spend money on an app like Clash of Clans, but these users spend so much money that sustains the business model. These users are sometimes referred to as 'whales' – they might spend thousands of dollars within a single game, sustaining the app developer and allowing the game to be free for all other users. Essentially this business model is the most successful because it casts a wide net, and as long as it attracts a few very large customers, a very large amount of profit can be made.

Understanding the types of apps viable and the corresponding business models to generate profit, your strategy should be to focus on games that are free to download and generate revenue through advertisements. It is very difficult to compete in the larger space of in-app purchase was driven games, as the market is mature enough that the product quality for market leaders requires a very large development cost. Games with ad revenue make money from every user, and it is unlikely that the net you cast with your app will catch any whales, so you will need each download to be profitable. It should also be clear that your app has to be free to garner downloads, as nearly no companies can release apps that cost money and still earn a good amount of revenue. Even the first Super Mario game to be released for phones did not generate as much revenue as initially thought – most analysts blame this on the fact that the app is locked behind a paywall instead of featuring in-app purchase with free content.

Building a Product

The business model to building your app is extremely important, as the rest of the process for building an app will largely be based on imitation. It does not matter if you have the greatest idea in the world for an original game if it does not have a catchy title and is immediately understood by potential users, it simply will not garner downloads. It cannot be overstated how many fantastic games are available on iOS and Android, but since a user is not familiar with the title or image behind an app, they simply cannot gain any traction and get downloads. This is going to be your challenge – you need to build momentum in your app to attract users, as the best marketing on the app stores is the top lists for downloads. Thankfully in recent years, they have distinguished many different top download lists, so you simply have to have success within your specific subgenre, instead of necessarily having a top downloaded 'game.' For example, if you make an app that rises in the sub-genre of puzzle games, this will be sufficient marketing.

It should be clear that your best bet at providing a steady stream of income will be from building a game for mobile devices, but I understand the desire to do something different. You might have a really good idea for an app, something that might even be quite revolutionary. I want you to consider two additional elements of app development. One, the cost to build something custom that networks to a central server are extraordinary. You can spend anywhere from ten to forty thousand dollars on this development, and then there is the upkeep required to run the app. This includes the fees for the server instruct, as well as the patches to keep the app updated with the latest version of mobile operating systems. Two, utility apps require a large amount of funding for advertising to get off the ground. There is a reason that people in their garage do not make successful utility apps – it requires lots of outside investment merely to get exposure. If you truly believe that you have a fantastic app in mind, I urge you to save that idea for a later time. You might be able to get it off the ground, but instead of coding your better bet would be making a business proposal and showing it to a venture capitalist firm. You will need too much money to get a utility app off the ground.

With building an app, you are starting from a place of either knowing how to develop for phones, or you do not. If you already have experience with programming, I suggest that you take a look at the popular development tools for phones, as these you probably have the require knowledge to make a compelling app yourself. There are established tools to help you make a game, such as Unity, and the cost to license this software is free – you must just pay royalties once you start generating revenue. You also have the option of hiring an app developer to help you create a program, and this is largely going to be how much of you create your first app.

If you do not have the technical skills to create an app, you can instead hire a programmer to build one for you. While they might use a program such as Unity to build the app, there are additional elements of optimization to get it to function properly on iOS and Android. The cost to hire an app developer to vary wildly based on what you are trying to accomplish. You are focusing on trying to create a stable revenue stream, and so I advise you to focus on games that run locally and require no server instruct. Any connectivity to a central server to statistics or to interact with other users requires more money than most individuals can afford. Moreover, the cost of app development rises exponentially when you focus on server connectivity – these app developers simply charge more because there are fewer developers with the specific set of skills necessary to make this work and work consistently.

To find a mobile developer, I would start with your social circle. Unlike other ventures, app developers are not a commodity. It requires such a specific set of skills that there is a huge variety in the quality of developers. As a general rule, American and European developers cost the most money, but you will also into fewer issues of language barriers. You will be giving specific instructions to a developer, so even if they are a fantastic coder, they might not be able to meet your specifications simply because they do not understand what you are trying to accomplish. If you cannot find someone to do it locally, or if they simply cost too much (a very real possibility), I would look to UpWork.com. You have to be *extremely careful* with the developer that you hire, as there is some extream variability in the talent of developers listed on this network. Many programmers only know C++ or JavaScript, and while these languages are useful, they will need to have experience with mobile development to be of any real use to you. Before you hire anyone, I suggest that you look at their past projects, specifically apps without networking features that were built in Unity; this would be the ideal developer. You will also want to make sure that they are charging enough. You do not want to hire the cheapest developer. If someone is charging less than $20 per hour, they are not going to be worth the money. The market is in desperate need of app developers, so the idea of someone charging a lower rate means that they aren't all that talented. In the long run, you will end up spending more money on an app because it will take significantly more time to complete the project.

Deciding what to Build

You know that the best way to produce a steady stream of passive income is going to come from games and not utility apps. The next question is what type of game you should build. You know that you want the game to run locally without any networking features, but also note that the game should be rather simple. Do not plan on creating a game in three dimensions for example, as this costs far more money and requires much more extensive bug testing. The more complicated the project, possible points of failure along the way. For what to build, look to popular two dimension games that are trending on the app store. You are trying this venture to create a revenue stream, not to express your ideas as a game developer. You will want to mimic the mechanics of popular games, and mostly just modify the assets used. For example, I have had some success with a Bejeweled Clone and also an Angry Birds clone. The idea of more or less copying someone's idea might seem repugnant, but truly this is the only way to get noticed on the App store. Original ideas just don't' make a lot of money.

If you are creating the app yourself, the process of imitation should be quite simple for you. You know what you are trying to accomplish and you already have the skills to do so. If you are hiring an app developer to build a game within Unity or some other game engine, you will need to create a design document. This is a list of instructions for the developer to follow and includes all aspects of what you want from the app. Creating a design document is not that hard, and essentially just requires two parts. The first part is writing down what a typical session with an app looks and feels like. You would detail what happens when a user launches the app, what the menus feature, and what a typical session looks like. You would then include the rules for your game. You can list that it is meant to function like Tetris or some other popular game, but you can't depend on a developer being intimately familiar with an existing game, even if it is well known. The second part of your design document is going to be full of images for each of the screens and seniors of your app. You would include a mock drawing of the menu screen, the main gameplay screen, and any additional scenarios that are central to the app you are creating. In these mock drawings, you will want to include where ads will be running on your app. This is quite essential to the get the resolution of the image right, as well as making sure the interface doesn't lead to a user accidently clicking on an advertisement. You might feel as though this would be a benefit to you, but you will make more money from a user repeatedly opening your app than having a user click on an ad, get annoyed, and then delete your game.

There will be a lot of back and forth between yourself and the app developer, and along the way, you will want to check their progress. The best way to handle this is to create a list of milestones for the developer to hit. You might not be familiar with how long each task should take to complete, but you should break down the essential steps for creating the application. Using an app when it is part way through development can be a bit tricky, and you will want to have your phone in a particular type of developer mode to test the app. This can be a complicated process if you are not very technical, so you will instead want the developer to send you a video of the app functioning. To give you an idea of some of the milestones a developer should meet, you want to make sure that they have a functioning menu screen, and then make sure that they have built in the basic features of the game, like the physics and making sure the game is running in real time. I've seen developers speed up the video on their apps to make it appear running faster than it does. This is a concern because if the optimization is not correct, you might have a great game that runs so poorly that no one will want to play it. Remember that you need users to not only download your game but also to repeatedly open it to gain revenue from advertisements.

How much will you make, and for how long?

It should be clear that advertisements are your main way of making money from any apps that you build. Adding advertisements to your app is a relatively simple process. If you are hiring an outside app developer, I would ask them to set up this feature for you, but even if you aren't the most technical person you can still get this feature running up quite quickly. You will want to simply research the different advertising firms that work with iOS and Android. If you are running an app on both operating systems, you are going to need to go through two different firms to get ads on both versions. I don't' want to recommend any firms in particular because what will differentiate most of them is how well their ads work within your particular app. For example, the total amount of screen space will differ by the firm, and depending on how well optimizing the app is that you create, you may need to refer to one firm over another. You will always want to run your app with the ads in place first to ensure that the added resources do not slow down what you made. This is a common occurrence and restricts the firms that app developers can use.

It is hard to say the exact amount of money that you will make from this venture, but there are a few predictors of revenue. For starters, the overall tail on games is fairly short once a game gets popular. It is highly unlikely that you create an app that a user will use for many months, as games simply have shorter tails than utility apps, even if they can gain users faster. You should expect that a moderately successful app makes around five to ten thousand dollars in six months. This is a fairly large sum of money, but this is a numbers game where you might have to put out five or ten games before you can expect that type of revenue. That being said, if you stick to the already mentioned formula of copying already popular apps, it increases your chance of success.

If you plan on making this a long term investment where you will be releasing many apps over the coming years, you should learn how to develop the apps themselves. You don't have to be a programmer, necessarily; you just have to become proficient at programs like Unity and learn the basics of scripting. You may still have to hire a developer to build a wrapper for the app and optimize your creations, but the cost of accomplishing these other goals is far less than if you are having a developer work on the app from beginning to end. You might think it very difficult to create games yourself, but truthfully as long as you are avoiding 3d games, you can learn it quite simply by looking at YouTube videos. This is merely another consideration, and if you find this to be a good source of revenue, I suggest you take the time to learn how to build the base product yourself.

Building on experience

Building your second and third apps will be much easier than building your first. That first app that you make requires a lot of research, and you have to think through the design document that you will be giving to an app developer. Once you have found an app developer that you can rely on, this whole process becomes much easier. I highly urge you to focus on finding one or two developers that you like to work with (if you are not building everything yourself) – in addition to knowing that they provide high-quality work, you also gain the experience of working with the same person repeatedly. This is a huge benefit in app development as gaining a developer that understands your design documents is quite difficult. You might be partnered with a fantastic programmer, but if he or she cannot understand your design documents, you will be paying for a lot of additional work to fix the errors created by miscommunication. Even if you think you are writing the clearest instructions imaginable, mistakes will be made, and teams work better together when they have experience working with each other.

Considerations

I emphasize that to master any single venture; it is necessary to find a mentor or teacher that can answer your questions directly. Above any other venture, this is no truer than when it comes to app development. I am extremely fortunate in that my brother is a programmer by trade. He didn't help me design any apps, but his guidance has been essential in getting my ideas off the ground. A mentor in app development can recommend developers, help you with your ideas, show you how to format a design document correctly, and more. You will have so many questions along the way, from designing physics models to understanding how close you can mimic a game without your app getting taken down. These are so specific that having a person to answer these questions directly will be immensely helpful.

You should also come to this venture with two to three thousand dollars to invest. You might not, and hopefully won't, use this on a single app, but you will want to have money put aside to finish any apps that you start. This is a huge problem in mobile development, where the costs to finish are simply greater than the starting investment. This is horribly unfortunate because it leaves an app designer with an incomplete product. If they do not have the technical expertise to complete it themselves, they will need money to pay a programmer to finish the project. An incomplete app will not earn any revenue, and so any money invested will essentially be lost. You must at least finish an app and release it to have any chance of creating a revenue stream – I know this is obvious, but I have read about this happening enough times that I want to mention it here.

As with all forms of passive income, you will have to pay taxes on any profit made from your apps. This is not a particularly difficult process as both Apple and Google have streamlined 1099 forms for profit made through the app store. It does become slightly more complicated when dealing with specific ad agencies, which is where most if not all of your revenue will be coming from. It is my suggestion that you find a tax accountant for when you file but note that the service they provide should be answering your questions for the first year that you make money from your apps. Filing in additional years, you should have the require information to do it yourself. There many people that participate in this market that file themselves, but I think it is worth the cost to have a tax professional help you with your first filing.

Chapter 10: Joint Venture Partnerships

What are Joint Venture Partnerships?

A joint venture partnership is when two companies come together so that they can use each other's resources, and then they both benefit. For example, a delivery company may hand out coupons from a manufacturer. The manufacturer gets free delivery of advertisements, and the delivery company will be the exclusive partner to the manufacturer. They are combining their resources to reduce costs and accomplish a goal that neither company could very easily accomplish on their own. While this is the legal definition of a joint venture partnership, for our purposes it will be slightly more expensive, including simply working with another party to pool your resources and make investments that neither party could accomplish on their own.

Your first opportunity at a joint venture partnership should be to promote your existing social media accounts. For example, in books one and two you learned how to earn passive income through Instagram and YouTube. Each account builds on the other, with subscribers from your Instagram account boosting your views on YouTube, and vice versa. This is just the tip of account synergy, and you should partner with other Youtube channels and Instagram accounts. There are some ways to do this, from engaging in larger competitions among the subscribers of both channels, as well as pooling resources on Instagram to get the notice of larger brands for product placement. This will merely offer the opportunity for free advertising but does not quite get at the heart of pooling resources for greater investment. To do this, you will need to partner with a close friend or family member and discuss possible ventures that you can both engage in together, but you would not be able to tackle alone.

In a joint venture partnership, you are not just pooling your monetary resources, but are also your labor. In the ventures for passive income listed below, keep this mind, both for your ability to participate in each venture, but also for the person that you will be working with. You need to trust your partner both regarding their financial commitment, but also their ability to provide labor for any single project. You might be able to gain the financial investment from a partner but find that they are unwilling to put in the labor. To avoid this, it is best to work with someone you know.

Do note that for most joint venture partnerships you have the opportunity to enter a legal agreement. I suggest that you do not do this. Regarding co-promote for your online ventures, this is simply unnecessary, as the income streams will be separate, and your partner will not be able to take over your account and lock you out. Regarding financial investment, a legal agreement might be necessary if you are partnering with someone that you do not know, but note that this adds quite greatly to the cost of starting a venture. You will have to hire a lawyer to write out the agreement, and theoretically, your partner will also have their lawyer review it. It adds a complication that isn't necessary if you are partnering with someone you know. Note that the projects mentioned here are largely local, which is what allows you to bypass a legal agreement. If you were engaging in ventures involving the stock market, this is a case where I would advise a legal agreement. The projects here are cases where it is quite easy to note that both parties are putting up equal investment, and both are splitting the revenue equally. It is harder to make these determinations when dealing with online income.

YouTube, Instagram, and EBook Promotion

The simplest form of a joint venture partnership is the promotion. If you already have made investments in YouTube, Instagram, and EBook writing, you will want to reach out to other entrepreneurs and to try and promote each other. This is more easily done with YouTube and Instagram, as I have not been very successful with promoting EBooks. You should find channels and accounts that are similar to yours since the user base is likely to be interested in both your material and your partner's. You will want to focus on channels and accounts that are similar in size to your own. You must make it clear that you both stand to gain subscribers and is by working together, and that you are not trying to leech their audience, something that could come to mind if your partner is more popular than yourself. This is true if you receive the offer to partner with a channel or account as well – make sure that they are about as popular as you, otherwise you are essentially offering a free promotion with very little in return. The audience size of your partner needs to be worth working together.

Conclusion

Thank you again for downloading Passive Income: Part Three.

If you have enjoyed the methods and strategies for generating passive income detailed in this book, please consider reading parts one, two, and four. In part four, you will continue to learn about how to generate passive income through small to modest monetary investments. If you have enjoyed the ideas presented in this book but lack the wealth to invest in these ventures, please refer to books one and two for methods of earning passive income with little to no financial investment. Building passive income is a process that builds on top of your past efforts, so all of this material will be relevant to building a strong stream of income.

You now have the methods and strategies to build passive income through financial investments. These are investments that require more of your money than your time, and to earn the income, you must merely wait for you investments to pay interest. I urge you to invest any interest that you earn back into these investments, as the more money that you dedicate, the greater your earnings potential. For the methods outlined in this book, I suggest that you start with peer to peer lending. More so than releasing an app or creating a joint venture partnership, this is a low-risk investment that requires little to no maintenance. The labor required is the upfront research to find potential candidates to lend money to, and the process of receiving payment is entirely handled through peer to peer lending sites.

All forms of earning passive income in this series will complicate your taxes in some fairly significant ways. This is particularly true with the ventures listed in parts three and four. I urge that you find a tax accountant when you file your taxes, at least for the first year that you are generating revenue. There are essential questions and details that they will be able to answer, and they will also be able to find deductions that you simply do not know about. This is the nature of more advanced investments – the earnings potential is large, but these ingrained investment opportunities also feature many nuances to your taxes. This is one aspect of passive income that I suggest you do not ask for help from a mentor or teacher if you decide to get one. How taxes are handled might be the same on a federal level, but the tax law in each state can vary wildly. Additionally, any income you earn could make you ineligible for certain benefits that you are receiving – this can be avoided by claiming profits at a later time, and is yet another reason to find professional help when filing your taxes.

Lastly, if you enjoyed this book, it would be much appreciated if you could leave a review on Amazon. The best way for this book to make its way into the hands of more readers is through truthful reviews about this work. Please write what you liked about this book and what could be improved upon. Any and all feedback is helpful as I continue to serve the needs of my readership.

Thank you and good luck!

Passive Income

Incredible Ideas of How to Make Money While You Sleep

Part Four

Passive Income Series

Part One:

- EBook Writing
- YouTube Ad Revenue
- Stock Photos
- Audio Samples

Part Two:

- Print per Demand
- Instagram
- Creating Online Courses

Part Three:

- P2P Lending
- Creating Apps
- Joint Venture Partnerships

Part Four:

- **Affiliate Marketing**
- **Informational Product**
- **Dividend Stocks**

Introduction

Passive income is one of the best forms of wealth. It is something that anyone can do and something that everyone will be able to benefit from. Whether you want to be able to make a lot of money or a little bit of money on the side of your full-time job, you can benefit from having some extra passive income in your life.

The idea behind passive income is that you put a decent amount of work in at the beginning of your project so that you do not have to worry about putting a lot of work (or any work, in some cases) into your business in the future. You will be able to simply sit back and collect the money that you worked hard for in the future. Now that you have read through each of the three previous books and you know what passive income is (along with the options that you have for passive income), you should be prepared to start making money.

This book will be all about three new ideas that you can use for passive income. These ideas are different than the last in that they allow you to make sure that you are going to be able to make the most amount of money. It will also allow you to try new things. While the previous books *did* have a good deal of options for people to be able to try when they are doing passive income, these ideas are ones that will bring about the most amount of money.

Having a lot of income at your disposal can be hugely beneficial. This means that you will need to make sure that you are going to be able to get the most out of the options that you have when it comes to your passive income experience. Some people even get so good at their passive income options that they can replace their full-time jobs. Can you imagine what it would be like to not have to work and just collect on money that you have earned? Passive income is amazing.

This last book in the series will have all of the extra tips that you need to make sure that you are making the most amount of money possible. It can sometimes be complicated when you are getting started so be sure to follow the tips in the best way possible. Hang onto the book and use it for reference even later on in your passive income career – you will be able to get a great deal of help from the different options that are included with it.

Just because you have the passive income doesn't mean that you won't have to worry about the different things that are going on. Try a combination of different passive income options and make sure that you are going to be able to get the most amount of money possible. This is a good idea especially in the beginning when you haven't quite found your niche yet. You may want to try many different things and see how they all work. It is a good idea to do this as long as these things don't take up *too* much of your time or cost a lot of money to be able to invest in.

Don't ever give up on the options that you have. You should make sure that you are always staying persistent and that you work until you get what you want out of the different options that are included in your passive income experience. You will not be able to start making money right away sometimes so try your hardest and make sure that you are going to be able to truly benefit from the experience and from the passive income resources that you have.

It can be hard to keep pressing on when you are first getting started and when you are struggling to make the money that you want but just remember your original dream and how great it will be to be able to relax and figure out what you are doing with your life after you have made that money. Let that motivate you and keep doing your best to make money. It will pay off, and you will be able to relax and enjoy the life that you have made for yourself with passive income.

The harder that you work when you are starting out with passive income, the more you will have when you are sitting back and collecting the money. For this reason, the passive income options get more and more difficult as you read through the books. These are perhaps the most difficult out of all of the options so make sure that you are prepared for the hard work that comes with each of them. Just know that it will pay off in the end and that you will be able to truly enjoy all of the different parts of it.

There are instructions that are included with each of the different options in your passive income guides. Be sure that you are following them and that you are working hard to make sure that you will be able to get the most amount of money possible. If you do not follow the instructions that are included with each of the options, you will not be able to get the best benefit possible. This will cause you to miss out on some of the money that you could be making, and it could make things harder for you when you should just be able to be enjoying your passive income without having to worry about doing more work.

There is some risk that will be involved with your passive income. The majority of the options are investments, and that can be risky on its own. Just make sure that you are prepared for your experience and that you are going to make sure that you are doing things the right way. If you take outrageous risks, you may not know the right way to do things, and you may end up missing out on different options for your passive income.

The most important aspect of making passive income is able to enjoy it. Know that you are going to make money, that you are going to be able to have a lot of money and that you are going to be able to relax with that money. Be prepared to make things better for yourself and to give yourself, even more, opportunities when it comes to the different options that you have. You will be able to truly get the most out of the passive income if you are prepared for what life is like with little work and a lot of money.

Most importantly: enjoy your passive income!

Chapter 11: Affiliate Marketing

Affiliate marketing is one of the easiest ways that you can start to make passive income. The most difficult aspect of it is that you need to set up the way that you are going to start offering the products that you are affiliated with. This means that you will need to put in some work to get into making money, but you will not have to worry about doing too much because the marketing part comes from other companies. It is not necessarily a part of your business but is more about the way that you can do different things within the business and the way that you can make sure that each of these things is going to be able to work with your business.

Costs

There are various costs that are associated with affiliate marketing, but the biggest cost that you are going to incur is the purchase of your website. You should have your domain name that will allow people to come to your site. This will also draw more people away from other sites and will give you the best experience possible for the blog when you are trying to do affiliate marketing.

Depending on the domain and the type of software that you are going to use, the cost that you are going to have to worry about will vary. It can be anywhere from around 50 dollars to about 1,000 dollars. The amount that you will pay will be different depending on what you are going to do with the website, the popularity of the name of your website and the software that you choose to use as the back office of your site. There are many different options that you can choose, and each of them will have an impact on the way that you choose to be able to make money from your blog.

A Short Time

Compared to some of the other passive income sites, it will only take you a short amount of time to be able to do the affiliate marketing portion of your site. You will just need to set the site up so that it is designed nicely, add some content to it and begin working on it with the information that you want. It is easy to set up a website, and you can even hire other people to write the blogs that are on the site (although, this will cost you slightly more money to be able to do).

After you have set it up, you can begin to get the followers that you need when you are working on the site. There are many different options for getting followers and making sure that you are getting the most out of it is the right way to be able to do things. It is a wise choice to make sure that you have a following on your website *before* you try to get people to buy your affiliate marketing. They will not be interested if you don't have a lot of people who know what your site is all about.

Setting Up a Blog

You will need to have a blog on your website if you want to be able to get traffic and if you want a way to communicate about the different things that are included with your affiliate marketing. It is easiest to make sure that you are going to be able to tell people about that information and that you are going to be able to get the most out of the experience when you do it.

If you are truly planning on making sure that you are going to be able to have the most amount of followers, your blog should be optimized to the information that is on your site. For example, if your site is all about doing DIY projects in your home, each of the blogs that you write about should have information about the way that you can do different things and the way that you can make sure that you are going to be able to add optional products to your blog. You should also make sure that you are letting people know that is what your blog is about and that you want to offer them product options so that they will be able to benefit from them in the same way that you do.

Making Your Name

You need to figure out a site name that is good for you. Make sure that you are going to learn the things that are important and are popular. There are many different options for your name depending on what your blog is about and the things that you are going to have on your site. The name of your site should be reflective of that and should be able to make the most amount of sense when it comes to the experience that you are going to be able to have. It is a good idea to try and make sure that you are going to be able to have the right experience for your blog and that you are going to be able to have followers on it.

Your name should be easy to remember, reflective of your business and popular according to what is common to the standards of the type of blog that you have. The name is what you will be known by and the blog is something that will be around for a long time if you know the right way to do it – make sure that your name is something that you will be comfortable with for a long time and is something that will be evergreen no matter what you choose to do with your blog and the things that you are going to have on your blog. The website name is just as important as the content that you have on your site and the information that you want to be able to put on the site.

Getting Followers

The only way that affiliate marketing companies will want to be able to use your site is if you have a lot of followers. This doesn't necessarily mean that you need to have the highest following in your blog category, but you should be working to make sure that people know who you are. What is the point of a blog if you don't have people who are going to follow you? There is none, and nobody will be interested in paying you to put their product on your site if they know that you don't have people who are reading the posts that you make.

There are several different ways that you can get followers. You can do it organically by simply asking people to look at your blog, or you can use search engine manipulation methods to be able to get people to come to your site. Do things like changing the words that are on the pages or adding different things that people will be able to see the first results in the search engines. The more hits that you can get on a search engine, the better you will be able to make sure that you are getting followers. The more people who see you, the higher the chance of people coming back to your site to read what you are talking about.

How You Can Profit

The way that you profit is similar to how people who own billboards profit. Companies will pay you money to be able to have their products on your site. The bigger and more popular your site, the more money that they will pay you. They want people to learn about their products and want people to buy them.

The other way that you can make money from the affiliate marketing is by listing the products on your page. When someone clicks on it and then buys it. As a result, you will get a percentage of the sale. This works similarly to commission and the way that people try to make money from commission. The companies that you do work with will only want to be able to pay you that amount of money if they know that you are going to be able to actually make money from it so make sure that you have a lot of followers and people who are reading your blog before you try to do affiliate marketing.

Getting Paid

You will be paid by the person who is selling the product. The chances are that you will get a check for the total amount that you have earned. This is the way that most affiliate marketing works and it is easy for you to get paid in this way.

There is also a chance that the seller of the object will also pay you electronically directly to your bank or in another way that makes use of a payment service.

It is always a good idea to try different things and to make sure that you are doing affiliate marketing in the right way. You should be sure that you know what you are doing and that you are going to be able to get the most amount of money possible from your experience. You don't have to worry about the different ways that affiliate marketing works if you just list the product and provide a link for people to be able to buy it. The money will start to come in just from you doing that.

Large Retailers

Affiliate marketing isn't just for small businesses or obscure companies that people have never heard of. While it is true that many people can get their name out in this way through the use of affiliate marketing, they are not the only ones who use it. They benefit from it in that they get more people to learn about them, but it is not exclusive to small businesses and strange companies that are relatively unknown.

Even large businesses and corporations will take advantage of affiliate marketing. Some have specific programs that are set up for people to be able to get the most out of the affiliate process and lead people to the site to be able to get more money from the products that they are helping to sell. It is a strategy that is used by many different businesses – both big and small – that will allow them to make the most use out of the different things that they are doing. It will also allow many business owners to be able to save some money on advertising because it is usually less expensive to pay an affiliate than it is to try to do some form of more traditional advertising.

Write Your Blogs

When you are writing the blogs that are going to go to your site, the number one thing that you need to do is make sure that they are relevant. Know that it is important that they cover the information that you want people to know. You should also know that it is a good idea to try and make sure that all of the blog information will be included with your blog. You won't have to worry about the problems that come along with your blog if you know the right way to write them.

Someone Else Writes Your Blogs

You can also pay someone else to write the blogs for your site. This will cost you more money upfront, but it will be worth it especially if the person who writes them knows what they are doing and can lead more people back to your site with a lot of traffic. It is always wise to try and have a professional do it. This investment can cost quite a bit of money, though, so be sure that you are prepared for that, and you are making sure that you have everything that you need to be able to do it.

Keeping Up with Traffic

Even after you get the traffic that you want when you first start, you will still need to make sure that you are going to have a lot of people coming to your site. You don't need traffic just at the beginning, and you should make sure that you are keeping up with the amount of traffic that you have so that sellers will always be wanting to put their products on your page. It is how you get paid so make sure that you are aware of the number of people who visit your page.

Tell People You're an Affiliate

Do not try to fool your audience or your readers with the affiliate marketing that you are doing. Some people may try to tell their readers to buy a product simply because they like it. You are not doing that as an affiliate marketer – you are showing it to them because you will be paid for it. Let them know. Most people will not care, but they *will* care if you try to sell them something and don't tell them that you are getting profit from it. Be honest, always and your readers will appreciate you more for it (and may even buy from you because of it).

Chapter 12: Informational Products

Creating informational products is yet another way that you can make passive income. These informational products are somewhat different from the things that you are going to do when it comes to other passive income options. This is because to create product information, you need to have some valuable information. You need to make sure that you are showing people the way that you can do things and teach them the right way to do it, too.

Deciding on Your Subject

You need to know that what you have is valuable. If you don't have something that is valuable, you will not be able to make money from it. It will be difficult to sell if it is not something that people are looking for then and you may not be able to make any money from it at all. It will lead to a wasted investment and the time and money that you have put into it will be gone.

The Information

There is a lot of information on a lot of different subjects. Learn the information that you need to know and that will lead to you being able to make sure that you are getting the most out of different situations. There are many different subjects that people are interested in, and when you learn about them, you can make sure that you are spending the most amount of time and money learning about something that can be different depending on what it is that people are looking for. It can sometimes be difficult to figure out what sells so be sure that you check all of the trends to get the right type of information.

When you are figuring out what you are going to teach people, you should make sure that you have all of the information on it. This is something that is essential because you don't want to leave information out. If you leave that information out and the people who have purchased the product find out, they will lose trust in your and there is a chance that they may not want the product or even return the product which will hurt your profit in a big way.

Only Experts

Only people who are technically considered experts should be putting product information on the Internet or anywhere. If you are just a novice, there is no way that you can teach people something even if it is as simple as Word skills. You need to make sure that you know what you can do and that you are confident with teaching other people the right way to be able to do it. Most people are experts at something, so you should figure out what that means for you and what you need to do to be able to sell that information.

How do you tell if you're an expert?

If you have to ask someone for help with something in your chosen subject or if you learn something new while gathering information from your chosen option, you are probably not an expert. While there is no way for a single person to know everything that they need to about their chosen subject, it is a good idea to make sure that you know a lot. Most experts know between 95 and 99% of the information that they need to about the thing that they are trying to teach other people about. Do you?

Figuring Out What Sells

You need to know what sells. If you know how to knit but people are more interested in die cutting, you won't be able to sell your knitting skills. This is especially true depending on the way that you do different things and the type of subject that you have when it comes to what you are going to teach about.

The easiest way to figure out what sells is to look at self-help and reference books on various charts. You can also watch videos online to get an idea of what you are going to be able to want to sell. Try different things until you find something that is popular, and that sticks so that you will be able to figure out what you need to sell and if any of your talents line up with what is popular at that time.

There are many different options to choose from when it comes to selling the information that you have. Just be sure that you choose something that is popular and that you know a lot about.

Getting Your Audience

You will probably need to do some advertising to get the audience that you want to your product information. Whether that is content marketing, email plans or traditional advertising through a grassroots movement will depend on what you are selling, how popular you think it is going to be and what you are selling. Different products will have different reasons for sales and different ways that you can make sure that the people are getting what they need. Be sure to choose the right way to get your audience so that you can get the biggest audience possible.

It is also important to make sure that you are getting the right *type* of people who you are marketing to. In general, you should find people who need your information, people who are capable of paying to get the information and people who are going to be able to benefit from the product that you have to offer. If you don't get the right type of audience to be able to market your information to, you will have a lowered ability when it comes to the options that are included with your information production for the audience.

Using a Website to Draw People In

You need to have a website that is going to draw people in. It doesn't matter how you plan to sell your information in the future or what you are going to do to be able to give your audience the information, without having that website, you will not be able to get an audience. This means that you need to make sure that you are going to be able to have the best audience possible and that there is some way for those people to connect with you. The website doesn't have to be anything special. You can simply use a basic format to be able to get the audience in, but that will enable you to have the site.

You can use website marketing and content to be able to show people what you have to offer. They will be able to find you on search engines and in other formats if you know the right way to market and if you do it properly on your site. You can try different things to get people to come to your website but knowing that you will almost always need a website can make it easier for you to be able to get what you need from your product information sales.

The Costs

Depending on the information that you are selling and the format in which you are going to sell it, you may have to pay a lot of money upfront to be able to sell the product to people. The costs can include the production of the information, setup of your website, and cost of a system to be able to sell the information on. These costs are about $1,000 and up but can be much more than that. If you have the skills to do some of the things on your own, it will cost you less than that.

Even though it will cost you some money to be able to start, you should know that you will be able to make that money back. It is not uncommon for you to make that much in a week when you are first getting started with the product information that you are selling. You can make sure that you make your money back by always trying your hardest and working to make sure that your information sells to the people who are going to be able to pay the most for it.

The Amount of Time

This is not a type of passive income that is only going to take you a few days to be able to set up. You need to make sure that you are prepared for a time investment that is nearly as large as your monetary investment. You should also be prepared to spend a month or more on getting things ready. This does not even account for the time that it will take you to become an expert (which can be years).

When you are going to start making passive income depends on how long it takes you to learn what you are trying to sell, set up the sales process, get the people who you need and start making your money back. The passive income will not count toward your profit and will not be worth it until you start to make back the money that you used to invest in the opportunity. It can sometimes take months to be able to start profiting. It is not uncommon for it to take a year or more to start profiting off of the things that you have made, though because of the way that things are set up for product information salespeople.

Showing Your Information

Always show the information that you have. Don't give away everything for free because there would no way to make money from it that way, but try to make sure that you are giving people a taste of what they will be able to get when it comes to the different options that are included with your product information. You can give them just a small portion of what you are going to be able to teach them and then let them know that they will have to pay to get the rest of it. This will entice them and make them want more.

If you give them just a little idea of what they can learn from your products, you will have a better chance at making sure that you are going to be able to do different things. You will also have a better chance at making that sale and allowing them to see that they are going to be able to do more with it. It can be a hard job to be able to get things done so try your best and just figure out exactly what you need to do to only give them a small taste of what you have to offer.

Websites

Since you are already going to have a website where you are going to build up the people who are going to buy your product information, you can go ahead and use it to sell the information. You can put the information that you are selling into a specific page on the site. The people who are on the site will need to have a password to be able to access it, and you can sell them the password. That is the way that you will make money from it.

The nice part of doing this is that you don't have to do anything extra to be able to sell your product information. The website should already be there, and you can simply add the password protected page to it with the information that your customers need to know. This is something that you can do without much training and something that you will probably not need a professional to do for you. If you are going to use a professional to build your site, you can simply have this added in as an option.

Videos

Another way that you can get people to get your information is by creating videos. They can pay for the videos on their own or buy them in a package. This will depend on the information that you are going to have to teach them, and that is something that is going to be different depending on the way that you do different things. Just make sure that you know the right way to secure the videos so that people have to pay for them. Otherwise, people may distribute them which will take away from the value of the videos that you have created because other people can just get them without having to worry about paying for them.

When you make a video, it can be easy to just put it on your site. This would be done in the same way that you put your individual text information on your site and will depend on the type of video that you have. While you can't necessarily sell your video on YouTube, you can use something like YouTube Red which is a subscription service and which you will get a cut of each time that you put a video on so that you can make money from it.

Authority Publishing

Similar to how you would write an eBook on something that you know a lot about, you can publish pages that are authoritative on the information that you are trying to give your readers. This is something that can be hard to do if you don't know how to create or publish books so make sure that you take a course or two on how to do it and that you use it to your best advantage when you are trying to make money from the download process.

It can sometimes be intimidating to be an authority publisher. Keep in mind that you are an expert on the information that you are creating so that people will be interested in hearing that information from you. You should make sure that you are always working hard to try different things and that you are teaching people each of these things when you are in different areas. It is a good idea to try things that are different from what you used to do and to try to add more value to your publications by being a true authority on the subject through your publishing options.

Paid Downloads

If you have valuable information, you will be able to ask people to pay to download the information that you have. Whether you put that into a PDF or some other type of document, you will be able to make sure that you are going to be able to get the most out of it and that people are going to be able to pay you for the information that you have. This is something that you can put on your website, on your social media profile or even on different types of platforms.

When you make the decision to do a download type of situation, you will be able to get the most out of it, and you will want to make sure that you are going to be able to bring a lot of valuable information to the people who download it. Always be sure that you are going to be able to add different things to the downloads so that people can get the most benefit out of it. If someone is going to pay for something that they are going to download, they should be getting as much as possible out of it.

Single Classes

Some people who are experts on information choose to offer classes to people who do not know the information. This is usually reserved for people who do not have a lot of information but what they do have is valuable to the other people who can use it. It is a good idea to figure out the right way to be able to offer that information and always to make sure that you are letting people know that the classes that you have are because you are an expert.

The easiest way for you to sell singular classes is to use a service like Udemy where you will be able to offer that information to the people who want to get it. There are thousands of people who use Udemy, and they will be able to find you among the information that you need to know. Despite the information that you have to offer and the things that you are going to be able to teach them, you should try to have at least one class on a service like this. It will help to get your name out and to get the information that they need to know in their hands. It is always a good idea to try and make sure that you are teaching them everything that you can in the span of one class so that you will be able to only ever make one class. As they continue to pay for the class, you will make money.

Courses

Similar to a single class, courses are designed so that they can be created beforehand and that people only have to download them. When you are designing the course, set up time frames for being able to make sure that you are going to get the most from it and that you will be able to profit off of it.

There are many different options that you have for designing courses, and when you do, you will be able to make sure that you are getting the most from it. You should include all of the information that you know about the subject and organize it in a way that is easy for people to learn from it. There are many different options when it comes to the way that the courses can be designed – find one that works for you and use it to be able to teach it to other people.

Chapter 13: Dividend Stocks

Dividend stocks are much smaller and easier to understand than their larger counterparts. This is something that even novice investors can do, and they have the possibility of building up a lot of money when it comes to the options that are included with investing. You can create a lot of passive income just from the dividends that are on the stocks that you have, and you will be able to enjoy the benefits.

While dividend investing may be the most expensive to start up, it is the passive income option that includes the least amount of work on your part. There is not a lot that you will have to do when you first start out, and there is certainly not a lot of work that you will have to do when you are continuing to make money from it.

How People Make Money with Dividend Investing

The idea behind dividend investing is that people can make money simply from the profits that come from the companies that they have invested in. This means that when you invest your money into a company, you will get a dividend of the profits that they have. Companies do this to not only give back to the people who have chosen to invest in them but also to make sure that they can save money on the taxes that they pay on the specific amount of money that they have paid. The more a company gives out in dividend payments, the less they have to worry about paying in taxes.

When you invest in dividends with a company, you will get a small percentage of the profits that they have. Despite the fact that it is small, you should still make some money. The amount that you invest will probably be far less than the amount that you can make off of it even though both of the amounts are relatively small.

The More Dividends, The Better

Most people who are able to truly profit from dividend investing do so because they have many different dividends investing streams that they have coming in. This means that they can make a lot of money from different sources.

For example, someone who invests in dividends may have invested in three different large companies. Even if they invested only a small amount, they can see big returns because there are three different streams of income that they have coming into them. It is a great way to make sure that you are making money and to get the most out of the money that you are making.

Finding a Company

There are many different companies that you can choose to invest in, and when you choose the right one, you will be able to make a lot of money from it. You will, in general, need to find a company that is offering dividend investing opportunities. This can be any company but should always be a company that is willing to let people invest in the different opportunities that they have. It can be difficult to figure out what you need to do or how much you need to invest so make sure that you find a company that is willing to help you with the options that you have.

When you are working to make sure that you are going to be able to invest, you should always find a company that is reputable and that makes a lot of money. If you don't, you could risk losing out on money that you would have been able to make from investing it in some other type of opportunity. Dividend investing is all about how much you can make and what you are willing to do to make that money.

Preparing to Invest

When you are getting ready to invest the money that you are spending on dividend investments, you need to make sure that you are fully prepared for it. You need to make sure that you have built up the amount of money that is required to buy into several different investment opportunities. You also need to make sure that you are prepared to make those investments. When you are preparing to invest, you should have money that you will be able to spend on the investment and money that you will be able to keep back in case of any incidentals.

You should also keep the information on the company close by so that you will be able to reference it when you are trying to make the investment. It may be hard to figure out exactly what you need to do with the investment, but you will be able to truly start to benefit when you know what you are doing and how much you will need to spend.

Cash Payments

The most common way that you will get paid on the dividend investment is through a cash payment. This doesn't necessarily mean that you will get cash in the sense that you would traditionally think of, but it does mean that you would be able to be paid through a check or an automatic deposit into a bank account. It is a good idea to try and make sure that you are going to be able to get the money in this way.

A company that is going to pay you in cash is a sign of a good company. When a business is financially healthy, they will be able to pay all of their investors in cash and not have to worry about how they are going to pay them. This is because they will have the cash flow that is needed to be able to pay everyone in the right way instead of just trying to pay them in different ways to make things work for them. It is a good idea to try and make sure that you know what you are going to be paying and how you can be paid.

Property Payments

Some companies may choose to pay their investors in property. This is great for a company that has been doing it for many years but can be a sign of financial instability if they suddenly switch from paying in cash to paying in the property. They may be trying to get rid of the things that they have stored, or they may simply need to find a different way to pay you because there are cash flow problems.

If you notice a company that you have invested in making a sudden change like this, pull out. Your money is likely not safe with the company, and you may end up losing money if you continue to stay with that company. There are many reasons to make sure that you are not keeping in with a company that has all of these problems but the biggest reason lies in that the company may be getting ready to fold and you will lose your money that you have invested in the process.

REITS

A real estate investment trust is a popular option for people who are investing their money in dividends. This is a company that owns a piece of real estate. All of the people who have invested in it come together as the owners. They do not necessarily make all of the decisions about the property, but they will get a cut of the profits on the property. It is a great way to ensure that you are investing in the right thing and that you will be able to make the right monetary decisions when it comes to different investing options.

The real estate investments that do the best are often the ones that are in big cities and have a lot of tenants. They make a lot of money and will always be needed because there is often not enough space for tenants in the cities. If you find a REIT in a smaller town, you may want to consider what you will be able to make off of it before you choose to put your money into it. It may not be as profitable as other REIT, and you may end up losing some of your investment money.

A Profitable Company

The company that you choose, no matter what type of company it is, should always be profitable. You can figure this out by looking at the publicly released trends on the company and any information that is put out by the tax office. It is a good idea to try to find different things on the company and learn as much as you can about it before you invest in it so that you will be able to make the most amount of money possible.

If you are going to make sure that you are getting what you can out of the investment experience, you should always have an idea of how the company has performed in the past. This doesn't mean that you need to just look at what the company puts out but also what has been released about it. You should always find a company that has not had losses in the past few years and a company that is going to be projected to keep profiting in the future. You need a company like this if you want to make real money from dividend investing.

No Major Problems

There could be major problems with a company that you may not even know about until you start taking a deeper look at the company. It is a good idea to try different things and find out as much as you possibly can before you make a choice to invest in the company. Look at the history and at any problems they may have had in the past so that you can learn what you need to about the company. It is also a good idea to try to make sure that you are going to be able to get what you can out of the company.

If the company has had any major problems in the past ten years, it can be a sign that things are going to go bad for the company in the coming years. This is not something that you will want to deal with while you are trying to make passive income so be sure that you are going to be able to have a company that is long lasting and that is not going to shut down at any point in the foreseeable future. You could have problems if the company is not able to bring money with you.

Yields on the Investment

The yields on the investment will be the amount of money that you make after you have made the decision to invest in the company. It is like your profit and will be the total amount that you made less the amount that you put into the business. It is a good idea always to keep track of the amount that you invested so that you will know how to figure out your yields.

If you can figure the way that the yields work, you can figure out the right way to make sure that you are going to be able to bring more attention to the money that you have made. You will also be able to make more money from the amount that you have invested in the different options that were included with your monetary assignments. Always do your best to make sure that you are yielding as much as possible and that you are going to be able to make the most amount of money from the options that you have. This is the only way that you can make true passive income from dividend investing.

Looking at Profits

The profit that you make from your dividend stocks will come directly from the profit that the company makes. This means that you need to make sure that you are going to choose a company that has a high amount of profits so that you do not have to worry about where your passive income is going to come from. The high profits should be long term and they should have a good trend to them that shows that the company will continue to make money no matter what happens with the economy.

A company that has been able to make money for a long time with no regards to the economy is one that is going to be worth the most for you. It will be easy for you to try and make sure that you are going to get the most out of it and that you will be able to truly enjoy the amount that you get. Passive income is all about having to do as little work as possible after you have put the initial work in and the right choice with dividend investing will allow you to get the most amount of passive income possible and the highest profits available so that you can truly enjoy your money.

Long Term

Dividend investing is great for the long term. Unlike the other types of investing for passive income, you will be able to truly enjoy the money that you make from your dividends for a long time. Most businesses that do well and have been doing well for years will continue to do well so that you can keep making money from them. There are many different ways that you can enjoy the benefits that come from long term dividend investing but make sure that you know how long this could be when you first get started.

If you are looking for a way to make a lot of money in a little time, dividend investing is not the best option for you. Even when it comes to other types of passive income, which can all take a long time, dividend investing is often the slowest with the returns. You should be aware of that before you start investing but also know that it will be able to benefit you in the long-term so that you can make the most amount of money possible and so that you can enjoy everything that comes along with the investment process.

Amount of Risk

There is not a huge amount of risk when you are investing in dividends. This is because the majority of the singular dividends are small investments. This means that you will not have to worry about how much you are going to spend because it does not take much to get started. Despite the fact that you do not need to take huge risks with dividend investing, you will still need to set aside some money for the investments that you are going to make.

Set aside money because it is hard to make a lot of money if you just invest in one dividend or you do not have a lot of money into it. It may be a good idea to only put a small amount into the investment when you are first getting started, but you will need to make sure that, if it works out for you, you are prepared to put even more money into it so that you can start to profit more. You can enjoy higher profits with the more amount of money that you buy into the investments with, and you won't have to worry about all of the problems that come with other dividend investing opportunities.

Your Passive Income

After you have made the right investment and have started to get a return on it, you will see that the passive income is worth it. No matter what type of investment you are doing or any other stream of work that you have done to make sure that you are getting passive income, you should be able to enjoy it.

Enjoying it, though, doesn't mean that you spend all of the money as soon as you get it because that could be a problem.

Instead, you need to make sure that you have a plan for your money. It could be to save the money, spend the money on things that will make more sense or simply do more with the money. You won't have to worry about where your next meal will be coming from when you have passive income, but you should be prepared to manage the wealth that you do have so that you do not have the problem of too much money.

Investing

One thing that is always a good idea when you are investing and you have passive income is to invest the money that you have made. It will be like making double the amount of money, and you can benefit from all of the aspects that come along with investments. For example, if you find that you are making a lot of money with dividend investing, you may choose to use some of the passive income that you have in your bank to be able to invest it in other opportunities. You can even try to invest it in other passive income opportunities. The more streams of income that you have, the better you will be able to make more money.

Now that you have gotten over ten different ideas of how to make passive income, you should have no problem choosing the one that works the best for you. It is always a good idea to try different things and to make sure that you are making the right decision so use this book to pursue as many opportunities as possible. Passive income is all about making a lot of money, figuring out the right way to invest your money and being sure that all of your money is going to the right things. You can truly begin to make good investment choices when you learn the right way to make passive income.

Conclusion

Passive income sounds like a lot of work, but it isn't as long as you are working to make sure that you are setting up the framework of the money that you are going to make in the future. When you can make passive income, you only have to do a lot of work at the beginning, and you don't have to worry about what kind of work you are going to do later on because you will just be collecting the money that you made from the work in the beginning.

Whether you are going to take the time to write a book, invest in something or build an application for your business or personal use, you will be able to enjoy the passive income. It can be fun to learn what to do and will give you the chance to be able to make a lot of money.

No matter what you have chosen, you can benefit from having read the entire series on passive income. There are many things that will help you to figure out the right way to do the things that are included in the series, and that will be able to help you figure out how to truly make passive income. Be sure that you take each of these options into account and that you can give yourself the best experience possible when it comes to the options that are included with the passive income choices in this series.

Passive income is so rewarding when you know what you are doing and can actually make money from it. Reading these books will have taught you everything that you need to know from the way that you can make money to the different things that you can do to ensure that you continue to make money well into the future.

Thank you for having read the entire series. You should now have a good idea of what is going on with passive income, how you can make money and the way that it works to be sure that you are going to get the most out of it. You can also benefit from the different options that are included with passive income and the way that it works.

Lastly, if you enjoyed this book, it would be much appreciated if you could leave a review on Amazon. The best way for this book to make its way into the hands of more readers is through truthful reviews about this work. Please write what you liked about this book and what could be improved upon. Any and all feedback is helpful as I continue to serve the needs of my readership.

Thank you and good luck!

Printed in Great Britain
by Amazon

83820149R00108